SOME THINGS YOU PROBABLY *DON'T* KNOW ABOUT ASPIRIN

• Americans swallow 80 million aspirin tablets a day—or over 29 billion pills annually (117 for every man, woman, and child).

• First aid for a heart attack might include aspirin. After calling 911, taking half an aspirin (crushed, chewed, or dissolved in water) may reduce damage and improve chances of survival.

• New research suggests that as little as one regular-strength aspirin every other day may cut the risk of death from colorectal, stomach and esophageal cancer by 40 percent.

• Aspirin appears to have a beneficial effect on immune responses. It boosts the body's production of natural cancer-fighting compounds.

• Aspirin may help stave off certain forms of senility by improving blood flow and preventing clots.

• You can't get high by combining aspirin and Coca-Cola, but new research suggests that the caffeine in Coke (or coffee) may be able to slightly boost the pain-relieving action of aspirin.

REDISCOVER ASPIRIN—
THE MODERN MIRACLE DRUG

Other Books By Joe and Teresa Graedon:

- **The People's Pharmacy** (St. Martin's Press, 1976; revised 1985)
- **The People's Pharmacy-2** (Avon Books, 1980)
- **Joe Graedon's The New People's Pharmacy: Drug Breakthroughs of the '80s** (Bantam, 1985)
- **50+: The Graedons' People's Pharmacy for Older Adults** (Bantam, 1988)
- **Graedons' Best Medicine: From Herbal Remedies to High-Tech Rx Breakthroughs** (Bantam, 1991)
- **No Deadly Drug** (Coauthored with Tom Ferguson—a medical mystery. Pocket Books, 1992)

Other Books By Dr. Tom Ferguson:

- **Medical Self-Care: Access to Health Tools** (Summit Books, 1980)
- **The People's Book of Medical Tests** (with David S. Sobel; Summit Books, 1985)
- **The Smoker's Book of Health** (G.P. Putnam's Sons, 1987)
- **The No-Nag, No-Guilt, Do-It-Your-Own-Way Guide to Quitting Smoking** (Ballantine Books, 1989)
- **Imaginary Crimes: Why We Punish Ourselves and How to Stop** (with Lewis Engel; Houghton Mifflin, 1990)
- **Helping Smokers Get Ready to Quit: A Positive Approach to Smoking Cessation** (Great Performance, 1990)
- **Hidden Guilt: How to Stop Punishing Yourself and Enjoy the Happiness You Deserve** (with Lewis Engel; Pocket Books, 1991)
- **What You Need to Know About Psychiatric Drugs** (with Stuart Yudofsky and Robert Hales; Grove Weidenfeld, 1991; Ballantine, 1992)
- **The Stethoscope Book & Kit** with Linda Allison; Addison-Wesley, 1991)
- **No Deadly Drug** (Coauthored with Joe Graedon—a medical mystery. Pocket Books, hardcover, 1992; Pocket Books Paperback, 1993)
- **The Get Well Quick Kit** with Linda Allison; Addison-Wesley, 1993)

The
ASPIRIN
HANDBOOK

A User's Guide
to the Breakthrough Drug
of the '90s

$\ominus \oslash \oplus$

by Joe Graedon, M.S.
bestselling author of
The New People's
Pharmacy
Tom Ferguson, M.D.
and
Teresa Graedon, Ph.D.

BANTAM BOOKS
NEW YORK   TORONTO   LONDON   SYDNEY   AUCKLAND

THE ASPIRIN HANDBOOK

A Bantam Book / July 1993

ISBN 0–553–56119–7

Published simultaneously in the United States and Canada

Bantam Books are published by Bantam Books, a division of Bantam
Doubleday Dell Publishing Group, Inc. Its trademark, consisting of the
words "Bantam Books" and the portrayal of a rooster, is Registered in U.S.
Patent and Trademark Office and in other countries. Marca Registrada.
Bantam Books, 1540 Broadway, New York, New York 10036.

PRINTED IN THE UNITED STATES OF AMERICA
RAD   0 9 8 7 6 5 4 3 2 1

ATTENTION

This book is not intended as a substitute for the medical advice of physicians. Although aspirin is available over the counter, it must be treated with respect. This is *not* a wimpy drug. No one should ever take aspirin, even in low doses, for extended periods of time without medical supervision. The reader should regularly consult a physician in matters relating to his or her health and particularly in respect to any symptoms that may require diagnosis or medical attention. Every reader must consult with his or her physician before starting or stopping any medication and before implementing any treatment discussed in this book. Most important, any side effects should be reported promptly to a physician.

ACKNOWLEDGMENTS

Readers of *The People's Pharmacy* newspaper column:
Who took the time to answer our questionnaire and send in special queries.

Toni Burbank:
A truly great editor! Ten years together is an eternity in publishing.

Charlote Sheedy:
A wonderful agent who helped make this project happen.

The Wonderful Folks at WJR in Detroit—
Warren Pierce & Terri Leib
The thousands of calls from WJR listeners helped inspire this book.

David and Alena Graedon:
Great kids who put up with their dad when he is on deadline.

Meredith and Adrienne:
For straight talk, open hearts, and unrelenting love, through good times and bad.

THIS BOOK IS DEDICATED TO:

Dr. Eva Salber:
An inspiring teacher and mentor whom none of us
will ever forget.

and

Dr. Lawrence Craven:
The first physician who had the wisdom to tell the
world that aspirin could prevent heart attacks and
strokes. Unfortunately, his colleagues weren't
paying attention.

TABLE OF CONTENTS

INTRODUCTION

Aspirin is the Rodney Dangerfield of the drug world. It just doesn't get the respect it deserves.

If scientists developed a brand new drug tomorrow that did even *one tenth* of the things aspirin does, people would stand in line and spend hefty sums to get their hands on the stuff. But because it's just plain aspirin, no one has been paying much attention.

We're convinced that this is about to change. Over the coming months and years, aspirin will be rediscovered as a modern miracle drug, perhaps the most versatile and extraordinary compound ever developed. That's why we decided to write this book.

The Aspirin Handbook is based on real questions from real people. We were lucky enough to have the input of literally thousands of concerned aspirin users—most of them readers of Joe and Teresa Graedon's syndicated newspaper column, *The People's Pharmacy*. An additional 400+ readers filled out our Aspirin Information Survey, listing their top questions and concerns about aspirin and related drugs. We have reproduced many of their questions in the text. Many thanks to all who helped.

ASPIRIN ADVANCES

In the 18 months it took us to research and write this book, new discoveries about aspirin have made this extraordinary drug even hotter than we had realized. During this brief period, studies appeared demonstrating that aspirin is useful in reducing the risk of colon and rectal cancer, preventing serious problems brought on by high blood pressure during pregnancy, lowering the risk of low-birth-weight babies, deterring migraine attacks, and diminishing the likelihood of heart attacks and strokes with mini doses (very low levels in the 30- to 75-mg range). We had to come back to the manuscript again and again to incorporate late-breaking research discoveries.

In addition, we discovered that there is a great deal of even more promising research in the works. Over the next few years, we may well be hearing announcements of other electrifying discoveries: aspirin to boost the immune system, aspirin against cataracts, aspirin to prevent gallstones, aspirin to reduce the risk of vascular senility, possibly even Alzheimer's disease. We only hope that doctors will be quicker to follow up on this new research than they were in using aspirin to prevent and treat heart attacks.

THE ASPIRIN SCANDAL

In 1989 the American medical establishment gave its seal of approval to aspirin, one a day, to prevent heart attacks in susceptible patients.[1] Forty years earlier a general practitioner, Dr. Lawrence Craven, in Glendale, California, was recommending to friends and patients that they take aspirin daily to lower their chances of a heart attack or stroke. Too bad it took so long for his colleagues to catch up.

Dr. James Dalen, editor of the *Archives of Internal Medicine*, speculates that if Dr. Craven's "rule of 'an aspirin a day' had been adopted by Americans in 1950, hundreds of thousands of myocardial infarctions [heart attacks] and strokes might have been prevented."[2]

Dr. Craven's published research was virtually ignored by cardiologists of his day. So was the observation by Dr.

Sidney Cobb that an unexpectedly small percentage (4 percent) of his rheumatoid arthritis patients died of heart attacks although the general population had a death rate from heart attacks of 31 percent. In his article in the *New England Journal of Medicine* in 1953, he attributed this surprising finding to the aspirin his patients had taken.[3]

By 1972 enough evidence had accumulated that a British heart specialist, Dr. Lee Wood, made so bold as to suggest that almost all adult men and women over the age of 40 should take an aspirin tablet daily. His exceptions were people with uncontrolled hypertension, those with an allergy to aspirin, people with bleeding disorders, and patients susceptible to bleeding ulcers. Writing in *The Lancet* he concluded, "The rationale for this regimen seems sound, the risks small, and the possible benefits enormous."[4]

Over the intervening decades Dr. Wood's recommendations held up amazingly well. If only more doctors had paid attention at the time! We hope that current research on other potential benefits of aspirin won't languish as long, but we fear that even when the results are in, it may take years for doctors to implement breakthrough discoveries.

Dr. Carl J. Pepine is editor-in-chief of the *Journal of Myocardial Ischemia* and chairman of cardiology at the University of Florida. He is angry that patients aren't being given aspirin at the first sign of a suspected heart attack although the data have shown for four years that this could save lives: "The bottom line is that patients are being deprived of necessary information concerning a very inexpensive, potentially life-saving medication . . . It would amount to malpractice to care for a patient with an MI [heart attack] without giving him or her aspirin." Dr. Charles Hennekens of Harvard Medical School agrees. "It should be the drug of choice, the first drug you give when they have a heart attack, but it's not. When it becomes so, I think we'll have saved 5,000 to 10,000 more lives in the U.S. each year . . . Sometimes I fear that if aspirin were half as effective and 10 times more expensive it would be taken far more seriously."[5]

For a detailed review of Dr. Lawrence Craven's unheralded discovery in 1948 turn to page 77.

We have no doubt that aspirin is a wonder drug that has been overlooked for far too long. We predict it will continue to dominate the headlines for the rest of the decade and far into the next century. Aspirin will at last get the respect it deserves and will no longer be confused with other pain relievers like acetaminophen or ibuprofen.

We trust that *The Aspirin Handbook* will help speed this process. Here's hoping that the chapters that follow provide useful guidelines for using today's—and tomorrow's—most popular, inexpensive, and beneficial drug.

Twenty Things You Probably *Didn't* Know About Aspirin

❑ **Americans swallow 80 million aspirin tablets daily—or over 29 billion pills annually (117 for every man, woman, and child).[6] The French prefer suppositories to pills. The Italians like fizzy forms of aspirin (comparable to Alka-Seltzer) and the British** go for aspirin powders that can be dissolved in water.[7]

❑ Willow bark, the precursor to modern-day aspirin, has been used for centuries to lower fevers and relieve pain. Chinese healers prescribed it in 500 B.C. One hundred years later Hippocrates told women in labor to chew willow bark to ease pain. The Greek physician Dioscorides gave willow bark to his patients for inflammation during the first century. The Bayer company finally began marketing aspirin in 1899.

❑ Doctors once cautioned women to shun aspirin if they became pregnant to avoid bleeding problems or complications during labor. Now many doctors are actually prescribing low-dose aspirin therapy (60 to 150 mg per day) for some high-risk pregnancies to reduce the danger of high blood pressure (preeclampsia and eclampsia) and lower the likelihood of babies with severely low birth weight.[8]

❑ It takes roughly 20 to 30 minutes for aspirin to be absorbed from the stomach and upper intestine into the bloodstream. Food slows down absorption. The peak effect occurs after about two hours and then slowly diminishes over the next several hours.

❑ You can't get high by combining aspirin and Coca-Cola, but new research suggests that the caffeine in Coke (or coffee) may be able to slightly boost the pain-relieving action of aspirin.[9]

❑ You can tell aspirin has started to deteriorate by smelling your open bottle. A vinegarlike odor indicates acetic acid, a breakdown product of aspirin.

❏ First aid for a heart attack might include aspirin. After calling 911, taking half an aspirin (crushed, chewed, or dissolved in water) may reduce damage and improve the chances of survival.[10]

❏ New research suggests that as little as one regular-strength aspirin per week may cut the risk of colorectal cancer in half.[11]

❏ Women who took aspirin 16 times or more per month and ate lots of fruits and vegetables had almost three times less colon cancer than those who ate few vegetables and avoided aspirin.[12] Men did almost as well (two and a half times less colon cancer). Researchers have known for years that aspirin and other arthritis drugs can block the development of polyps and tumors in animals fed cancer causing chemicals.[13,14]

❏ Aspirin appears to have a beneficial effect on immune responses.[15] It boosts the body's production of natural cancer-fighting compounds like interferon and interleukin in the body.[16]

❏ In test tube experiments aspirin reduces the spread of flu viruses.[17] Research in animals has demonstrated that aspirin enhances antibody response after influenza vaccination.[18]

❏ One quarter of an aspirin daily (75 mg, or roughly one baby aspirin) has been shown to reduce the risk of heart attacks in patients with angina by 34 percent.[19]

❏ Healthy male physicians who took one regular-strength aspirin every other day had 44 percent

fewer heart attacks than their colleagues who took
no aspirin.[20]

❑ Male physicians at high risk for heart attack because of chronic chest pain (stable angina) were able
to cut their risk 87 percent by taking one standard
aspirin every other day.[21]

❑ One million Americans have atrial fibrillation, a
type of heart rhythm disturbance that quintuples
their risk of stroke (leading to 75,000 extra strokes
each year). Many do not even realize they have this
irregularity and are vulnerable to strokes. One standard aspirin daily appears to cut their risk of stroke
by about 50 percent.[22]

❑ Tiny aspirin doses (30 mg, or less than one tenth
of a regular pill) have been shown to be as effective
as higher doses in preventing strokes and heart attacks after patients suffered transient ischemic attacks (TIAs) or minor strokes.[23]

❑ One aspirin every other day has been shown to
reduce the likelihood of a migraine attack by 20
percent.[24]

❑ Aspirin may help stave off certain forms of senility. Vascular or multi-infarct dementia is caused
by lots of little blood clots in the brain. It is more
common than previously believed.[25] Aspirin may help
prevent vascular dementia.[26] It keeps blood from
clotting, improves blood flow, and helps people do
better on tests of thinking ability.[27]

❑ People with Alzheimer's disease may also benefit
from aspirin. Canadian researchers have been ex-
ploring the possibility that this brain disorder could

be caused in part by a destructive inflammatory condition brought on by an immune reaction.[28] They have proposed that anti-inflammatory drugs like aspirin or corticosteroids may play a role in prevention or treatment of Alzheimer's disease.

❑ A number of studies have raised hopes that aspirin therapy may reduce the risk of cataract formation in the eyes.[29,30,31,32] Much more work is needed to confirm this observation since there are also data that contradict this finding.

HOW TO USE THIS BOOK

(1) Reading through Part I will help you focus in on the uses of aspirin that may be of most concern to you. You will also learn about the incredible range of aspirin doses—from 30 mg to prevent blood clots to as much as 8,000 mg daily to fight an acute attack of rheumatic fever. We'll give you the latest news on the best dose for a variety of benefits, as well as information on who should not take aspirin.

(2) In Part II you will find a discussion of the traditional uses of aspirin, plus some new ones. Some of the latter are very well established and can be put into practice immediately. Others are still experimental, but tantalizing.

(3) As great as aspirin may be, it also has potentially serious side effects. Learn about the complications and how to recognize a problem before it becomes life threatening. Find out how to reduce your risks in Part III.

(4) Part IV gives you practical guidelines on choosing a brand—or purchasing aspirin in its generic form. There are an amazing number of different kinds of aspirinlike drugs on the market, some of which are much less likely to cause stomach problems.

(5) People who experience difficulties with aspirin or who can't tolerate it at all will want to consult Part V to learn about a variety of alternatives to aspirin. Arthritis victims may be surprised to learn that acetaminophen (**Anacin-3, APAP, Panadol, Tylenol,** etc.) may provide better relief than expected.

(6) In the back of this book you will find several useful appendices. They list over-the-counter drugs containing aspirin, acetaminophen, and ibuprofen and provide critical information on other drugs that interact dangerously with aspirin and acetaminophen.

No one should ever take aspirin for granted. If you are planning to rely on this useful drug for longer than a few weeks, make sure you check in with your doctor first. Monitoring is critical for anyone on regular aspirin therapy.

References

1. At the Second American College of Chest Physicians (ACCP) Conference on Antithrombotic Therapy.

2. Dalen, James E. "An Apple a Day or an Aspirin a Day?" *Arch. Intern. Med.* 1981; 151:1066–1069.

3. Cobb, Sidney, et al. "Length of Life and Causes of Death in Rheumatoid Arthritis." *N. Engl. J. Med.* 1953; 249:533–536.

4. Wood, Lee. "Treatment of Atherosclerosis and Thrombosis with Aspirin." *Lancet* 1972; 2:532–533.

5. Hurley, Dan. "A New Battleground in the Aspirin Wars." *Medical World News* 1992; 33(Dec.):28–30.

6. Colleen Cotter, The Aspirin Foundation. Personal communication, Dec. 28, 1992.

7. Dolan, Carrie. "What Soothes Aches, Makes Flowers Last, And Grows Hairs?" *Wall Street Journal,* Feb. 19, 1988, p. 1.

8. Imperiale, Thomas F., and Stollenwerk Petrulis, Alice. "A Meta-analysis of Low-Dose Aspirin for the Prevention of

Pregnancy-Induced Hypertensive Disease." *JAMA* 1991; 266:261–265.

9. Schactel, B.P., et al. "Caffeine as an Analgesic Adjuvant. A Double-Blind Study Comparing Aspirin with Caffeine to Aspirin and Placebo in Patients with Sore Throat." *Arch. Intern. Med.* 1991; 151:733–737.

10. ISIS-2 (Second International Study of Infarct Survival) Collaborative Group. "Randomised Trial of Intravenous Streptokinase, Oral Aspirin, Both, or Neither Among 17,187 Cases of Suspected Acute Myocardial Infarction: ISIS-2."; *Lancet* 1988; 2:349–360.

11. "Aspirin Cuts Cancer Risk." *Medical Tribune* 1992; 33(Dec. 12):1.

12. Thun, Michael J., et al. "Risk Factors for Fatal Colon Cancer in a Large Prospective Study." *J. Natl. Cancer Inst.* 1992; 84:1491–1500.

13. Rosenberg, L., et al. "A Hypothesis: Nonsteroidal Anti-Inflammatory Drugs Reduce the Incidence of Large-Bowel Cancer." *J. Natl. Cancer Inst.* 1991; 83:355–358.

14. Bishop, Jerry E. "Aspirin May Cut Risk of Dying of Colon Cancer." *Wall Street Journal,* Dec. 5, 1991, pp. B1–B12.

15. Baron, John A., and Greenberg, E. Robert. "Could Aspirin Really Prevent Colon Cancer?" *N. Engl. J. Med.* 1991; 325:1644–1645.

16. Hsia, J., et al. "Aspirin and Thymosin Increase Interleukin-2 and Interferon-Gama Production by Human Peripheral Blood Lymphocytes." *Immunopharmacology* 1989; 17:67–73.

17. Huang, Richard T.C., and Dietsch, Ellen. "Anti-Influenza Viral Activity of Aspirin in Cell Culture." *N. Engl. J. Med.* 1988; 319:797.

18. "Aspirin the Wonder Drug: It Shows Promise for Everything from Gallstones to Cancer." *Consumer Reports on Health* 1991; 3(10):73–76.

19. Juul-Moller, S., et al. "Double-Blind Trial of Aspirin in Primary Prevention of Myocardial Infarction in Patients with Stable Chronic Angina Pectoris." *Lancet* 1992; 340: 1421–1425.

20. The Steering Committee of the Physicians' Health Study

Research Group. Preliminary Report: Findings from the Aspirin Component of the Ongoing Physicians' Helath Study." *N. Engl. J. Med.* 1989; 318: 262–264.

21. Ridker, Paul M., et al. "Low Dose Aspirin Therapy for Chronic Stable Angina: A Randomized, Placebo-Controlled Clinical Trial." *Ann. Int. Med.* 1991; 114:835–839.

22. Stroke Prevention in Atrial Fibrillation Study Group Investigators. "Preliminary Report of the Stroke Prevention in Atrial Fibrillation Study." *N. Engl. J. Med.* 1990; 322:863–868.

23. The Dutch TIA Trial Study Group. "A Comparison of Two Doses of Aspirin (30 mg vs. 283 mg a Day) in Patients After a Transient Attack or Minor Ischemic Stroke." *N. Engl. J. Med.* 1991; 325:1261–1266.

24. Buring, Julie E., et al. "Low-Dose Aspirin for Migraine Prophylaxis." *JAMA* 1990; 264:1711–1713.

25. Skoog, Ingmar, et al. "A Population-Based Study of Dementia in 85-Year-Olds." *N. Engl. J. Med.* 1993; 328:153–158.

26. Larson, Eric B. "Illnesses Causing Dementia in the Very Elderly." *N. Engl. J. Med.* 1993; 328:203–205.

27. "Aspirin and Multi-Infarct Dementia." *Physicians' Drug Alert* 1989; Aug.:58.

28. McGeer, Patrick L., and Rogers, Joseph. "Hypothesis: Anti-Inflammatory Agents as a Therapeutic Approach to Alzheimer's Disease." *Neurology* 1992; 42:447–449.

29. Seddon, J.M., et al. "Low-Dose Aspirin and Risks of Cataract in a Randomized Trial of US Physicians." *Arch. Ophthalmol.* 1991; 109:252–255.

30. Sharma, Y.R., et al. "Systemic Aspirin and Systemic Vitamin E in Senile Cataracts: Cataract V." *Indian J. Ophthalmol.* 1989; 37:134–141.

31. Mihail, S. "Aspirin in the Preventive Treatment of Cataract." *Oftalmologia* 1990; 34:43–46.

32. Harding, J.J., and Heyninger, R. "Drugs, Including Alcohol, That Act as Risk Factors for Cataract, and Possible Protection Against Cataract by Aspirin-Like Analgesics and Cyclopenthiazide." *Br. J. Ophthalmol.* 1988; 72:809–814.

I

ASPIRIN AND YOU

CHAPTER 1

SHOULD YOU TAKE ASPIRIN?

☐ **Aspirin relieves pain and inflammation.** Millions of people benefit daily from aspirin. It provides them with relief from the pain of arthritis, tendonitis, headaches, backaches, muscle strains, and other injuries. You can pay 20 times more for a pricey prescription anti-inflammatory agent, but you can't get better pain relief. Aspirin is the gold standard.

How Aspirin Fights Pain

Although this drug has been used to ease pain for nearly 100 years, it wasn't until the early 1970s that a reasonable theory was advanced to explain aspirin's pain-relieving mechanism. Sir John Vane received a Nobel prize for his hypothesis. The redness, swelling, heat, inflammation, and pain associated with trauma are caused in large measure by hormonelike chemicals called prostaglandins. These compounds are formed from a precursor chemical called arachidonic acid, which is found in a variety of cell membranes. Injury (a sprain, strain, burn, or blow) releases these irritating substances from local tissue.

Aspirin blocks an enzyme (prostaglandin synthase, or cyclooxygenase) that the body uses to convert arachidonic acid into a variety of prostaglandins. Reduction in levels of these prostaglandins is thought to relieve pain, fever, and inflammation. Aspirin isn't the only compound that works this way. A family of other aspirinlike drugs, known as nonsteroidal anti-inflammatory drugs (NSAIDs), do much the same thing. They include ibuprofen and prescription medications like **Clinoril, Feldene, Naprosyn**, and **Voltaren**.

For the last twenty years Vane's prostaglandin theory held center stage. But a new and more comprehensive theory is surfacing that may better explain aspirin's ability to fight pain. Dr. Tony Yaksh is a professor of anesthesiology at the University of California at San Diego. In 1992 he and a colleague reported that an important contribution of aspirin and other anti-inflammatory agents occurs at the level of the spinal cord, not just at the *site* of the injury or inflammation.[1] They discovered that aspirin-type drugs help dampen pain sensations by preventing nerve activation in the spinal cord and possibly even within the brain. So even after 100 years scientists are still working to unlock aspirin's secrets.

❑ **Aspirin helps prevent heart attack and stroke.** Low daily doses of aspirin, perhaps even small amounts (75 mg or less[2]), can help people with heart disease prevent heart attacks and strokes. This drug can also help prevent heart attacks in healthy people. Aspirin may thus be the best—and cheapest—insurance policy money can buy.

Dr. Lewis Thomas (author of *The Lives of a Cell* and *The Medusa and the Snail*) is quite likely our greatest living physician-philosopher. In his newest book, *The Fragile Species,* he offers the following observation: ''My own theory is that the 20 percent drop in American coronary disease was the result of commercial television, which appeared in the early 1950's and has made a substantial part of its living ever since through the incessant advertising, all day and all night, of household remedies for head-ache and back pain, all containing aspirin."[3]

❑ **Aspirin: first aid for heart attack.** For someone having a heart attack, aspirin may be one of the first and best lines of defense. Many paramedic teams now carry aspirin in the ambulance and hospitals often give aspirin in the emergency room to a patient experiencing symptoms of a myocardial infarction (MI).

A person who develops crushing chest pain needs to act quickly. Every second counts. Dr. Michael V. Vance, president of the American Board of Emergency Medicine, recommends to people who believe they are suffering a heart attack, **"Call 911, then take an aspirin."**[4] Actually, half a tablet, "crushed or chewed for a rapid antiplatelet effect," is the recommendation from ISIS-2 (Second International Study of Infarct Survival).[5] The ISIS-2 researchers studied 17,187 patients in 417 different hospitals worldwide. When aspirin was taken immediately upon suspicion of a heart attack and continued for 30 days, the death rate dropped by 23 percent; when it was combined with the clotbuster streptokinase, the numbers were even more startling—43 percent fewer deaths.

The blood-thinning action of aspirin starts within minutes and "has a profound antiplatelet effect within one hour."[6] Aspirin may partially help open up constricted arteries or prevent further blockage and thereby help salvage compromised heart tissue. Dr. Carl J. Pepine is editor-in-chief of the *Journal of Myocardial Ischemia* and chairman of the cardiology department at the University of Florida. In an editorial in his journal Dr. Pepine offers the following commentary: "Think how many lives might be saved if, for example, a bottle of aspirin were a standard item in first-aid kits—whether in airplanes, sports stadiums, or any other public place—or if people experiencing symptoms of a possible heart attack knew to take an aspirin while waiting for an ambulance to arrive."

Some people should never take aspirin, even if they *are* having a heart attack. Those who are allergic to aspirin, people with uncontrolled hypertension, bleeding disorders, severe ulcers, or a tendency to hemorrhage should avoid aspirin unless it is administered by a physician.

❑ **Aspirin helps prevent colon and rectal cancers.** There are over 150,000 cases of colon cancer diagnosed each year in the United States. Over 60,000 people die annually from this disease, making it one of the most common and lethal malignancies we face. Anything that could reduce the risk of this disease would be a miracle medicine.

Aspirin is that miracle. Animal research and human epidemiology confirms that aspirin has a dramatic effect on colorectal cancer. Four different investigations have confirmed that regular low-dose aspirin use can cut colon cancer deaths in half.[7,8,9,10]

One of the reports, published in the *New England Journal of Medicine,* was headed by Michael J. Thun, from the American Cancer Society. He and his colleagues examined data from 662,424 people in an American Cancer Society ongoing investigation. A six-year follow-up analysis published in the *Journal of the National Cancer Institute* (October 7, 1992) noted that men and women who ate lots of fruits and vegetables and also took at least 16 aspirin tablets a month had a phenomenal track record. They had an almost threefold reduction in colon cancer deaths compared to those who consumed low-fiber foods and avoided aspirin.[11]

The moral of the story: Eat your veggies, chomp those fruits, go for high-fiber grains, and talk to your doctor about regular aspirin, especially if there is a family history of colorectal cancer. As little as one regular-strength aspirin pill per week may provide substantial benefit.[12] By the way, acetaminophen (**Anacin-3, Panadol, Tylenol**, etc.) produced no such protective effect. In fact, there was a slightly (not statistically significant) increased cancer risk associated with acetaminophen use.[13]

❏ **Aspirin reduces the risk of some problem pregnancies.** Once upon a time, not very long ago, doctors warned women to stay away from aspirin during their pregnancies. There was great fear that aspirin would increase gestation time, prolong labor, complicate delivery, and raise the risk of hemorrhage both for mother and newborn. Nowadays obstetricians are actually prescribing low-dose aspirin (60 to 150 mg per day) in some high-risk pregnancies in order to lessen complications and improve the outcome for mother and newborn.

The problem is high blood pressure. For reasons that are not at all clear, many women (5 to 15 percent) experience hypertension during their pregnancies. This condition used to be called toxemia of pregnancy (preeclampsia and eclampsia). It can lead to puffiness in the hands and face, hard-to-treat fluid retention, electrolyte imbalance, kidney problems, epilepticlike seizures, coma, and death for the fetus or mother. Pregnancy-induced hypertension can be a life-threatening condition.

Enter aspirin. A "meta-analysis" of six different studies concluded that "low-dose aspirin reduces the risks of PIH (pregnancy-induced hypertension) and severe low birth weight, with no observed risk of maternal or neonatal adverse effects."[14] The numbers were phenomenal—a 65 percent reduction in high blood pressure and a 44 percent reduction in severe low birth weight in newborns.

No pregnant woman should consider aspirin therapy on her own. This is not a do-it-yourself project. But if there is a history of toxemia, the potential benefits of aspirin should certainly be discussed with an obstetrician who has kept up with the latest developments.

❏ **Aspirin leads to fewer migraines.** Everyone knows that aspirin is effective against ordinary headaches. But killer headaches, like migraines, were never thought to benefit from aspirin. It would be, the experts thought, like trying to kill flies with a feather. One of the totally unexpected findings of the Physicians' Health Study (involving 22,000 healthy male doctors) was that the men taking regular low-dose aspirin (one tablet every other day) experienced approximately 20 percent fewer migraine headaches than those on placebo.[15]

This result didn't show up until later data analysis because the study was designed primarily to detect reduction in heart attacks (which were indeed reduced by 44 percent). The researchers who analyzed the data concluded that "migraine is mediated, at least in part, by the effects of platelets [the sticky cells in blood] and suggest that low-dose aspirin should be considered for prophylaxis among those with a history of established migraine."[16]

FUTURE POSSIBILITIES FOR ASPIRIN

❑ **Aspirin may help prevent cataracts.** Physicians still aren't certain what causes cataracts, the most common cause of blindness worldwide. There is a growing belief that oxidative damage from highly reactive compounds called free radicals clouds the lens. Exposure to sunlight (ultraviolet radiation) or cortisone-type drugs seems to accelerate the process.

Natural antioxidant compounds like vitamin E, vitamin C, and beta carotene (a precursor of vitamin A that is found in orange vegetables, greens, and many fruits) appear to offer some protection against cataracts. Research has shown that people with low levels of vitamin E and beta carotene in their blood are more likely to develop cataracts, while individuals with high levels of these antioxidants are less likely to have such problems.[17] Aspirin also appears to possess antioxidant action.[18] In addition, it affects sugar metabolism and other biochemical processes that may be important in cataract formation.

Starting in 1981, a number of epidemiological studies showed that aspirin use may help protect against cataract formation.[19,20,21,22] Regular users of aspirin (especially those with rheumatoid arthritis) had roughly half the cataract surgery of nonusers. Unfortunately, other epidemiological research has not confirmed these benefits. This may be in part because cataracts evolve over a lifetime and short-term studies of less than five years may not be adequate to detect an effect.

A recent editorial in the British journal *Lancet* summarizes the current situation: "The balance of evidence is inconclusive, but the question needs to be resolved. If any drug were able to reduce the morbidity due to cataract, the sum of its benefit would be enormous, and aspirin is the best candidate going. The definitive answer requires a well-planned prospective trial over at least 5 years; this should be undertaken now."[23]

❑ **Aspirin and improved immunity.** Who wouldn't want a stronger immune system? What with cancer, AIDS, and all sorts of other nasty environmental threats out there waiting to pounce, one would theoretically jump at anything that could improve resistance.

New research has shown it may actually be possible to boost immunity. A placebo-controlled study of older people found that a standard multiple vitamin supplement improved several measurements of immune function. The levels of natural killer cells, T-cells, and interleukin-2, and the antibody response were all better in the vitamin takers. They also experienced half as many sick days as their non-vitamin-taking counterparts.[24]

Can aspirin also provide improved immune response? No one has yet done a really good study to answer that question, but there are some tantalizing tidbits that give us hope. Dr. Judith Hsia at George Washington University found that aspirin "significantly enhanced production" of the body's natural infection fighters, interferon and interleukin-2.[25] She is now looking at aspirin "to improve flu shot responses. The reason we are doing this is that there are large segments of the population that are not getting good protection from vaccination, especially the elderly and people with chronic medical problems like diabetes or HIV infections. Of course these are the very people who need to have the best protection against flu."[26]

It is still far too early to suggest that aspirin will help your immune system or improve antibody response to influenza vaccination. But stay tuned, this could be one of the next aspirin breakthroughs.

❑ **Will aspirin prevent gallstones?** It is estimated that 10 percent of adults in western, industrialized countries are likely to have gallstones sometime in their lifetime. Most of these stones (80 percent) are made up of cholesterol. When the bile in the gallbladder gets too rich in cholesterol, the cholesterol can form crystals that may encourage gallstone growth.

One of the key elements in this process is gallbladder mucus. It is the excessive production of this mucus that is thought to accelerate cholesterol crystal growth, which ultimately leads to gallstones.[27] Researchers have discovered a unique animal model for studying this disease. When prairie dogs were put on high-cholesterol diets, they developed gallstones. Large doses of aspirin prevented excessive mucus creation and gallstone formation.[28]

It is far too early to assume that aspirin will also work for people. But good data does suggest that 300 mg of aspirin daily can reduce mucus formation by the gallbladder in humans. The researchers conclude that "This action is consistent with a role for aspirin in the prevention of gall stones."[29] Unfortunately, preliminary studies have been contradictory. While some have suggested that aspirin can prevent stones, other studies have demonstrated no effect.

It will take a long-term commitment to well-controlled research before we can tell the true story of aspirin and gallbladder disease. Until that work is completed, don't count on aspirin to save you from gallstones. One way to prevent such problems, though, is to convert to vegetarianism, since vegetarians rarely develop gallstones.[30]

❑ **Aspirin and Alzheimer's disease.** Over four million Americans suffer from one of the cruelest of all illnesses. Alzheimer's disease is a mind slayer, robbing people of their personalities, their memories, and their joy of life. Researchers are still a long way from unlocking the secrets of this dread disease or coming up with a cure. But in the meantime, how about preventing it in the first place?

Dr. Patrick McGeer is a professor of psychiatry at the University of British Columbia in Vancouver. He is one of Canada's foremost researchers in the field of Alzheimer's disease. In 1990 the National Institute on Aging invited Dr. McGeer and other leading Alzheimer's researchers to Bethesda, Maryland, for a brainstorming session. These experts were told to "stick your necks out."

Dr. McGeer described his research on inflammatory mechanisms in Alzheimer's disease. He has found that damage to brain cells may be caused in part by "immune-mediated autodestructive processes."[31] In other words, the body is tricked into attacking its own nervous system. What really electrified the assembled scientists was his suggestion that "an aspirin a day might keep the gerontologists away." Dr. McGeer pointed out that anti-inflammatory agents could play an important role in prevention: "Maybe the best one is aspirin. I've never seen a rheumatoid arthritis patient with signs of Alzheimer's on autopsy."[32]

In a subsequent letter to the editor of the journal *Lancet*, Dr. McGeer reported on a preliminary study that showed a low level of this disease in patients with rheumatoid arthritis. He concluded that the data "suggest that the prevalence of Alzheimer's disease in patients with rheumatoid arthritis is unexpectedly low and that anti-inflammatory therapy might be the explanation."[33]

It would be wonderful if the story ended there. But a quick follow-up report by scientists at the Mayo Clinic could not confirm Dr. McGeer's observations.[34] Much more research will be required before anyone can start thinking about taking aspirin to prevent or treat Alzheimer's disease. Fortunately, Dr. McGeer has started that work.

WHO SHOULD TAKE ASPIRIN?

So what does this mean for you? In brief, a significant proportion of the adult population of the United States should probably consider talking to their physicians about the benefits of aspirin. For the following groups, aspirin may be especially helpful.[35,36,37,38]

- Patients with coronary artery disease
- People with angina
- Individuals at risk of coronary artery disease
- Smokers (who are by definition at risk)
- Patients with transient ischemic attacks (TIAs or mini strokes)
- People with a history of thrombotic stroke (due to a blood clot)
- People having a heart attack
- Those with a family history of heart attack or thrombotic stroke
- Pregnant women who have had hypertension in a previous pregnancy
- People with a family history of colorectal cancer
- Individuals with recurrent migraines
- People with arthritis

Again, in all the cases mentioned above, aspirin should be used only with medical supervision!

References

1. Malmberg, A.B., and Yaksh, T.L. "Hyperalgesia Mediated by Spinal Glutamate or Substance P Receptor Blocked by Spinal Cyclooxygenase Inhibition." *Science* 1992; 257: 1276–1279.
2. Juul-Moller, S., et al. "Double-Blind Trial of Aspirin in Primary Prevention of Myocardial Infarction in Patients

with Stable Chronic Angina Pectoris." *Lancet* 1992; 340: 1421–1425.

3. Thomas, Lewis. *The Fragile Species*. New York: A Robert Stewart Book/Charles Scribner's Sons, 1992.

4. Hurley, Dan. "A New Battleground in the Aspirin Wars." *Medical World News* 1992; 33(Dec.):28–30.

5. ISIS-2 (Second International Study of Infarct Survival) Collaborative Group. "Randomised Trial of Intravenous Streptokinase, Oral Aspirin, Both, or Neither Among 17,187 Cases of Suspected Acute Myocardial Infarction: ISIS-2." *Lancet* 1988; 2:349–360.

6. ISIS-3 (Third International Study of Infarct Survival) Collaborative Group. "ISIS-3: A Randomised Comparison of Streptokinase Vs. Tissue Plasminogen Activator Vs. Anistreplase and of Aspirin Plus Heparin Vs. Aspirin Alone Among 41,299 Cases of Suspected Acute Myocardial Infarction." *Lancet* 1992; 339:753–770.

7. Rosenberg, L., et al. "A Hypothesis: Nonsteroidal Anti-Inflammatory Drugs Reduce the Incidence of Large-Bowel Cancer." *J. Natl. Cancer Inst*. 1991; 83:355–358.

8. Kune, G.A., et al. "Colorectal Cancer Risk, Chronic Illnesses, Operations, and Medications: Case Control Results from the Melbourne Colo-Rectal Cancer Study." *Cancer* 1988; 48:4399–4404.

9. Rosenberg, L., et al. "Response." *J. Natl. Cancer Inst*. 1991; 83:1183.

10. Thun, Michael J., et al. "Aspirin Use and Reduced Risk of Fatal Colon Cancer." *N. Engl. J. Med*. 1991; 325:1593–1596.

11. Thun, Michael J., et al. "Risk Factors for Fatal Colon Cancer in a Large Prospective Study." *J. Natl. Cancer Inst*. 1992; 84:1491–1500.

12. Late News. "Aspirin May Cut Colon Cancer Risk by 50 Percent." *Medical World News* 1992; Nov.:9.

13. Thun, Michael J., op. cit., 1991.

14. Imperiale, Thomas F., and Petrulis, Alice Stollenwerk. "A Meta-Analysis of Low-Dose Aspirin for the Prevention of Pregnancy-Induced Hypertensive Disease." *JAMA* 1991; 266:261–265.

15. Buring, Julie E., et al. "Low-Dose Aspirin for Migraine Prophylaxis." *JAMA* 1990; 264:1711–1713.

16. Ibid.

17. Knekt, Paul, et al. "Serum Antioxidant Vitamins and Risk of Cataracts." *Br. Med. J.* 1992; 305:1392–1394.

18. Woollard, A.C., et al. "Antioxidant Characteristics of Some Potential Anticataract Agents." *Free Radic. Biol. Med.* 1990; 9:299–305.

19. Cotlier, E., and Sharma, Y.R. "Aspirin and Senile Cataracts in Rheumatoid Arthritis." *Lancet* 1981; 1:338–339.

20. Van Heynigen, R., and Harding, J. "Do Aspirin-Like Analgesics Protect Against Cataracts? A Case-Control Study." *Lancet* 1986; 1:1111–1113.

21. Mohan, M., et al. "India-US Case-Control Study of Age-Related Cataracts." *Arch. Ophthalmol.* 1989; 107:670–676.

22. Harding, J., et al. "Protection Against Cataract by Aspirin, Paracetamol and Ibuprofen." *Acta Ophthalmol.* 1989; 67: 518–524.

23. Editorial. "Preventing Cataract." *Lancet* 1992; 340:883–884.

24. Chandra, Ranjit Kumar. "Effect of vitamin and trace-element supplementation on immune responses and infection in elderly subjects." *Lancet* 1992; 340:1124–1127.

25. Hsia, J., et al. "Aspirin and Thymosin Increase Interleukin-2 and Interferon-Gama Production by Human Peripheral Blood Lymphocytes." *Immunopharmacology* 1989; 17:67–73.

26. Barbour, John. From Associated Press Newsfeatures. Jan. 19, 1992.

27. Lee, Sum P. "Editorial: Lessons from Experimental Cholelithiasis: Gallbladder and Mucosa, Nonsteroidal Antiinflammatory Drugs, and Gallstones." *Gastroenterology* 1991; 101:857–860.

28. Lee, S.P., et al. "Aspirin Prevention of Cholesterol Gallstone Formation in Prairie Dogs." *Science* 1981; 211:1429–1431.

29. Rhodes, M., et al. "Inhibition of Human Gall Bladder Mucus Synthesis in Patients Undergoing Cholecystectomy." *Gut* 1992; 33:1113–1117.

30. Pixley, F., et al. "Effect of Vegetarianism on Development of Gallstones in Women." *Br. Med. J.* 1985; 291:11–12.

31. McGeer, Patrick L., and Rogers, Joseph. "Hypothesis: Anti-Inflammatory Agents as a Therapeutic Approach To Alzheimer's Disease." *Neurology* 1992; 42:447–449.

32. Pollner, Fran. "Alzheimer's Disease: Experts Pursue Plethora of Drugs." *Medical World News* 1990; Feb. 12:16–17.

33. McGeer, Patrick L., et al. "Anti-Inflammatory Drugs and Alzheimer's Disease." *Lancet* 1990; 335:1037.

34. Beard, C. Mary, et al. "Rheumatoid Arthritis and Susceptibility to Alzheimer's Disease." *Lancet* 1991; 337:1426.

35. Resnekov, L., et al. "Antithrombotic Agents in Coronary Artery Disease." *Chest* 1989; 95:52S.

36. Sherman, D.G., et al. "Antithrombotic Therapy for Cerebrovascular Disorders." *Chest* 1989; 95:140S.

37. Dalen, James E. "An Apple a Day or an Aspirin a Day?" *Arch. Intern. Med.* 1991; 151:1066–1068.

38. "Aspirin, The Wonder Drug." *Consumer Reports on Health* 1991; 3:73–76.

CHAPTER 2

HOW MUCH ASPIRIN SHOULD YOU TAKE?

One of the most extraordinary things about aspirin is the fact that at different dosages, aspirin works in very different ways. There are very few medications that exert a powerful pharmacological effect when given at one twentieth the standard dose. Aspirin's daily dosage can vary from 30 mg per day (to prevent heart attack or stroke), to 650 mg (for a garden variety headache), all the way up to to to 8,000 mg per day (to treat an acute flareup of rheumatic fever). That represents a 266-fold difference.

To visualize this incredible spectrum, imagine taking one standard aspirin tablet which contains 325 mg. Smash it to bits with a spoon. Now extract one tiny chunk—about one tenth of a tablet. That represents roughly 30 mg. Compare that to 24 tablets (8,000 mg) and you begin to get an idea of aspirin's flexibility. No other medicine provides such an impressive variety of benefits over such a wide range of doses. To get the appropriate effect, though, you have to take the proper dose.

Here is a quick overview of what happens if you take (1) a tiny dose, (2) a low dose, (3) a regular dose, or (4) a large dose of aspirin. For more details, see chapters 4 through 10.

Mini-doses (30 to 81 mg—1/10 to 1/4 of a tablet per day)

- Prevents blood clots
- Prevents heart attacks
- Prevents strokes
- Treats heart attacks
- Prevents and treats 'mini-strokes' (TIAs).

Low Doses (325 mg—one tablet daily or every other day)

- Prevents heart attacks
- Reduces the chances of arterial leg surgery
- Prevents migraine headaches
- Prevents colon cancer
- Prevents rectal cancer

Standard Doses (325 mg to 650 mg—one to two tablets every four hours)

- Helps relieve most non-migraine headaches
- Relieves pain
- Reduces fever
- Prevents mini-strokes (TIAs)
  (one to four pills as prescribed by M.D.)

High Doses (3,600 mg to 6,000 mg—eleven to twenty tablets per day)

- Reduces inflammation from most causes
- Controls the pain and inflammation of rheumatoid arthritis
- Treats gout
- Treats rheumatic fever

MINI-DOSES (30 TO 81 MG PER DAY)

By any standard this has to be considered a super-low dose of aspirin. We are talking about one tenth to one-fourth of a standard aspirin tablet—one twentieth to one eighth of the usual headache dose.

Most people have a very hard time believing that such a small amount of aspirin could do anything. We have bought into the "lottle" principle: If a little is good, we figure, then a lot'll be better. This "more is better" attitude is likely linked to advertising. Marketing mavens have discovered that Americans love words like *extra strength, arthritis strength,* and *maximum strength.* The idea that **minimum strength** might be best seems mind-boggling.

Since it is impossible to knock out a headache with a baby aspirin tablet of 81 mg, most folks (and many physicians) find it beyond comprehension that such a small amount could work to prevent strokes or heart attacks. Yet recent research suggests *half* a baby aspirin may exert powerful anticlotting effects and help prevent many cardiovascular complications.

How can this be? Scientists have discovered that aspirin affects two chemicals produced within our bodies: *thromboxane A_2* and *prostacyclin.* Thromboxane makes blood platelets stickier, so they are more likely to clump together in a clot. It also makes blood vessels squeeze down smaller. Prostacyclin provides the balance, making platelets less sticky and opening the vessels, promoting a freer flow of blood. As a consequence, prostacyclin appears naturally helpful in preventing the conditions that might trigger heart attacks and strokes.

Researchers have assumed that the more prostacyclin you have and the less thromboxane A_2, the better off you would be. The trouble is that at standard doses aspirin is indiscriminate. It can halt the body's ability to make both chemicals. The good guys get zapped along with the bad guys. But in mini-doses, in the 30- to 75-mg range, aspirin appears to knock out the clot-maker thromboxane without affecting our friend prostacyclin.

New research confirms that 30 mg is just as effective in preventing minor strokes (transient ischemic attacks, or TIAs for short) as bigger doses and is less likely to cause side effects.[1] Half a baby aspirin may be the best dose of all to prevent heart attacks, strokes, or other cardiovascular complications, but only future research will tell for sure. Platelets have a relatively short life span (about eight days), so it is necessary to keep taking aspirin regularly to keep new platelets from sticking together to form clots.

LOW DOSE (ONE 325 MG TABLET)

Many of the largest aspirin studies utilized "low dose" formulations. One regular-strength (325 mg) aspirin tablet has to be considered a low dose, since it is half the normal quantity recommended for headache relief or to reduce a fever. But this amount of aspirin, taken either daily or every other day, has proven itself extraordinarily effective in preventing heart attacks, transient ischemic attacks (TIAs or small strokes), migraine headaches and various circulatory problems.

One study of 87,678 female nurses tracked aspirin consumption over six years. The nurses swallowed aspirin "sporadically" for problems such as headaches, muscle strains, and mild arthritis. The women who took one to six tablets per week had a 32 percent reduction in the risk of heart attack compared to those who consumed no aspirin.[2] One interesting anomaly was the discovery that women who took more than six tablets of aspirin per week did not appear to reduce their risk of a heart attack. Whether this was a statistical fluke or an important discovery remains to be determined.

Men appeared to fare even better on low-dose aspirin. The Physicians' Health Study initially reported a 44 percent reduction in heart attacks in healthy men taking one 325-mg tablet every other day.[3] Follow-up analysis revealed that those who were at high risk of heart disease (those with chronic unstable angina—translated as hard-to-treat chest pain) were able to reduce their risk of heart attack as much as 87 percent.[4] Such a reduction is nothing short of miraculous.

Additional analysis of the Physicians' Health Study uncovered other unexpected benefits of alternate day aspirin use. Researchers found that circulatory problems in arms and legs were substantially reduced in aspirin takers. Surgery was far less common in these people.[5] Migraine victims also seemed to benefit from alternate day aspirin treatment. They had a 20 percent reduction in attacks.[6] The investigators speculate that migraines are triggered when platelets clump together and release a neurochemical called serotonin. For some, aspirin seems to prevent the process from starting.

REGULAR DOSE (TWO 325-MG TABLETS)

The standard aspirin dose of two tablets has been used for almost 100 years to treat fevers and relieve pain from arthritis, headaches, toothaches, backaches, and almost any other ache you can think of. It is based on the old apothecary measure of 10 grains.

What is a grain? you might ask. This ancient weight standard was based on a plump grain of wheat. One grain equals 64.8 mg; hence, 10 grains of aspirin amounts to 648 mg. Half that dose, or 324 mg, is the exact 5-grain amount in a regulation aspirin tablet. Now you don't have to be a pharmacist to realize that this is an odd and somewhat unwieldy number. Consequently, most drug companies put 325 mg in their pills to make them seem more normal.

HIGH DOSE (11 TO 20 325-MG TABLETS PER DAY)

Standard aspirin doses generally will not calm the inflammation of severe arthritis or relieve the symptoms of rheumatic fever. For such conditions physicians prescribe the equivalent of anywhere from 12 to 18 regular tablets a day. An acute flare-up of rheumatic fever may temporarily require as many as 24 tablets to overcome the heart inflammation and fever.

At such high doses scientists believe that aspirin suppresses hyperactivity of the immune system. Neutrophils, a type of white blood cell, are defenders against bacterial or viral infections. They attack the invaders by releasing toxic chemicals and enzymes. Unfortunately, these same enzymes (proteases), peptides, and peroxides can damage tissue and irritate joints in autoimmune diseases like rheumatoid arthritis. High doses of aspirin prevent neutrophils from attaching to cell membranes. As a result, these irritating chemicals are not released and inflammation is eased.

References

1. The Dutch TIA Trial Study Group. "A Comparison of Two Doses of Aspirin (30 mg vs. 283 mg a Day) In Patients After A Transient Ischemic Attack or Minor Stroke." *N. Engl. J. Med.* 1991; 325:1261–1266.
2. Manson, JoAnn E., et al. "A Prospective Study of Aspirin Use and Primary Prevention of Cardiovascular Disease in Women." *JAMA* 1991; 266:521–527.
3. The Steering Committee of the Physicians' Health Study Research Group. "Preliminary Report: Findings from the Aspirin Component of the Ongoing Physicians' Health Study." *N. Engl. J. Med.* 1989; 318:262–264.
4. Bankhead, Charles D. "More Data on Aspirin as MI Shield." *Medical World News* 1991; January: 12–13.
5. Goldhaber, Samuel Z., et al. "Low-Dose Aspirin and Subsequent Peripheral Arterial Surgery in the Physicians' Health Study." *Lancet* 1992; 340:143–145.
6. Buring, Julie E., et al. "Low-Dose Aspirin for Migraine Prophylaxis." *JAMA* 1990; 264:1711–1713.

CHAPTER 3

WHO SHOULD *NOT* TAKE ASPIRIN?

As with any drug, one must weigh potential benefits against potential hazards. Excitement about aspirin's worth must always be tempered by the realization that aspirin carries substantial risks and is not for everyone. Nobody should ever undertake long-term aspirin therapy without medical supervision and regular monitoring.

ASPIRIN ALLERGY

Allergy seems so mundane that it may be hard to take it seriously. After all, there are 30 million Americans who suffer from hay fever and countless millions more who are allergic to cats, dust mites, perfume, mold, mildew, and goodness knows what else. Many of these poor souls pop an antihistamine or snort a decongestant and continue on their way. They may complain a lot (justifiably, in our opinion), but we rarely consider their condition life threatening.

Don't be fooled. Aspirin allergy is dangerous. Just as penicillin allergy can result in anaphylactic shock (breathing shutdown and cardiovascular collapse) and death, so too can aspirin allergy. For susceptible individuals, even a baby aspirin can bring on symptoms. Breathing problems (bronchoconstriction), itchy red hives, generalized rash, fluid retention, and shock are all possible signs of this reaction.

❏ **Asthma patients are particularly vulnerable.** People with asthma, nasal polyps, or a history of hives have to be extremely cautious with aspirin. In our opinion they should never take aspirin unless it has been specifically prescribed and supervised by a physician who knows about their allergic sensitivity. Not all such individuals will get into trouble, but a surprisingly high number (up to one fifth) will react to aspirin with runny nose, shortness of breath, wheezing, or other breathing difficulties. Skin rash and hives are also frequent complications in these highly primed patients.

Sometimes the symptoms come on suddenly, within minutes of exposure. But this allergic reaction can also be insidious and emerge gradually after several hours. An asthma sufferer may not realize that his breathing problems were brought on by the aspirin that was taken hours before. Even when aspirin does not make asthma worse, it may contribute to nasal polyps. These grapelike growths in the nose can be quite unpleasant and may require surgical removal. For all these reasons, aspirin allergy must be taken very seriously.

There is one other group of patients that should avoid aspirin because of hypersensitivity. People who have developed allergic symptoms while taking anti-inflammatory drugs like diclofenac (**Voltaren**), fenoprofen (**Nalfon**), ibuprofen (**Advil, Motrin IB, Nuprin,** etc.), indomethacin (**Indameth, Indocin**), ketoprofen (**Orudis**), meclofenamate (**Meclofen, Meclomen**), naproxen (**Anaprox, Naprosyn**), and others could cross-react to aspirin. In other words, if you have once experienced allergic symptoms from a nonsteroidal anti-inflammatory drug (NSAID), be forewarned that you may react to all other similar drugs in the same way.

ASPIRIN AND STROKES

One of the most controversial and confusing issues regarding regular aspirin therapy relates to the risk of stroke, otherwise known as a CVA (cerebrovascular accident). What makes this so complex is that there are two different kinds of strokes. Aspirin clearly lowers the likelihood of one kind while quite possibly elevating the danger of the other.

❑ **Aspirin prevents clotting (thrombotic) strokes.** Let's start at the beginning. Many strokes are caused by blood clots that lodge in an artery that feeds the brain. These blood clots can start almost anywhere that atherosclerotic plaque builds up, such as carotid arteries or even coronary arteries. Blood clots can occur in other places as well. People with a special kind of heart rhythm irregularity called atrial fibrillation are at high risk of developing small blood clots in the heart. All that it takes to bring on a stroke is for a fragment of a blood clot to break loose and lodge in the brain.

There is now a substantial body of research that proves aspirin can help reduce the risk of thrombotic strokes, especially for those who are at highest risk—patients who suffer TIAs (transient ischemic attacks, or minor strokes) or have atrial fibrillation.[1,2,3,4,5,6,7] The doses that have been shown to be effective against strokes or TIAs range from 30 mg to 1,300 mg (four tablets) daily.[8,9] Researchers are still trying to determine the amount of aspirin that is optimal against thrombotic stroke.[10]

❑ **Aspirin and bleeding (hemorrhagic) strokes.** As effective as aspirin may be at preventing strokes caused by blood clots, there is concern that it could actually increase the risk of the other kind of stroke, known as hemorrhagic or bleeding stroke. When a blood vessel in the brain breaks, blood pours out into brain tissue. This can lead to cat-astrophic results. Although this type of stroke is less common than thrombotic stroke, it can be equally des-tructive.

Aspirin does have the ability to "thin the blood," mak-ing platelets less sticky. People who take a lot of aspirin sometimes bruise more easily. This could be considered a kind of hemorrhage in which the blood vessels break or allow blood to leak into surrounding tissue.

Experts have been debating the question of whether as-pirin poses a danger of bleeding strokes for years. The Physicians' Health Study of 22,000 doctors initially re-ported a slightly higher risk of hemorrhagic stroke in men who took one aspirin every other day.[11] Although the trend was not statistically significant, the editor of the *New England Journal of Medicine,* Dr. Arnold Relman, warned of the risk of brain hemorrhage in an editorial. A follow-up analysis of the data published one year later re-ported somewhat less concern.[12] Canadian researchers "noted an increasing rate of hemorrhagic stroke in the Province of Quebec, Canada, and are concerned that this rise may be due in part to increased consumption of aspirin."[13]

Other studies have shown that low dose aspirin treatment is associated with an extremely low risk of hemorrhagic stroke or perhaps no risk at all.[14,15] This has led one re-viewer to conclude that "it is not possible to claim that the last word has been written on the subject, but it is unlikely that aspirin poses a risk of any consequence in causing hemorrhagic strokes."[16]

Until the final word *is* in, however, we encourage cau-tion. People with uncontrolled hypertension appear to be at special risk and should not take aspirin. Anyone who has had a bleeding stroke or who has a history of hem-orrhagic stroke in the family should also avoid aspirin un-less told specifically by a physician that such therapy is appropriate.

REYE'S SYNDROME

❑ **The debate is over.** There is no longer any serious doubt that aspirin poses a risk of Reye's syndrome when it is given to children or teenagers who have chicken pox or influenza. Although this condition is extremely rare, it is fatal in 20 to 30 percent of cases and can lead to permanent brain damage in children who manage to survive. Symptoms include irritability, personality changes, vomiting, lethargy, delirium, and ultimately coma.

Every bottle of aspirin now comes with a warning: "CHILDREN AND TEENAGERS SHOULD NOT USE THIS MEDICINE FOR CHICKEN POX OR FLU SYMPTOMS BEFORE A DOCTOR IS CONSULTED ABOUT REYE SYNDROME, A RARE BUT SERIOUS ILLNESS REPORTED TO BE ASSOCIATED WITH ASPIRIN." To read that you would think there had never been a fight over this issue, but you have no idea what a controversial hot potato this was a decade ago. Many physicians as well as representatives of the pharmaceutical industry disputed the connection. The FDA waited quite a long time before requiring a warning on the label.

Epidemiologist Devra Lee Davis and her colleague Patricia Buffler have calculated that 1,470 excess deaths may have occurred during the five years (1981 to 1986) the Food and Drug Administration debated adding a warning label about Reye's to aspirin containers.[17] Once the warning label about Reye's syndrome was placed on aspirin bottles the incidence of this potentially deadly disease dropped dramatically.

The problem with this warning is that parents can't always tell if their children have the flu or just a bad cold. Chicken pox starts out with a mild fever and general blah feelings. It may take one to two days before the skin rash appears. Since early diagnosis can be difficult, the safe thing to do is administer either acetaminophen or ibuprofen to children or teenagers who have a fever unless the doctor specifically recommends aspirin.

BLEEDING DISORDERS

Anyone with a tendency to bleed should avoid aspirin unless a physician has specifically given the green light and is carefully monitoring progress. This means that aspirin is contraindicated for people with hemophilia, bleeding ulcers, or any other hemorrhagic condition. Anybody on anticoagulant medication such as **Coumadin** (warfarin) must avoid aspirin like the plague. Those with a history of cerebral aneurysms should also stay away from this drug.

People with diabetes and eye complications that result from this disease should also avoid aspirin unless a physician is prescribing it and carefully supervising treatment. The fear is that aspirin might increase the risk of hemorrhage within the eye, although there is one study that suggests aspirin may actually reduce certain complications of diabetic retinopathy.[18]

SURGERY

❑ **Surgeons fear aspirin.** The risk of hemorrhage can make operations more complicated. Postoperative bleeding can also be a serious problem. People who anticipate surgery must always check with the surgeon and anesthesiologist in advance to see if and when aspirin should be discontinued. The recommendation is often made to stop aspirin one to two weeks prior to hospitalization so that bleeding complications during and after surgery can be minimized.

PREGNANCY

Although there is growing evidence that aspirin can help prevent pregnancy-induced hypertension and reduce the risk of severely low birth weight babies, pregnant women should never take this drug without an obstetrician's supervision. There are risks associated with aspirin during pregnancy, including prolonged gestation, anemia, longer labor, and hemorrhage during and after delivery. That's why every bottle of aspirin comes with the following warning: "IT IS ESPECIALLY IMPORTANT NOT TO USE ASPIRIN DURING THE LAST 3 MONTHS OF PREGNANCY UNLESS SPECIFICALLY DIRECTED TO DO SO BY A DOCTOR BECAUSE IT MAY CAUSE PROBLEMS IN THE UNBORN CHILD OR COMPLICATIONS DURING DELIVERY."

Medical textbooks warn that when aspirin is taken close to delivery, there is greater danger of stillbirths and neonatal deaths. Newborns and nursing babies can also be adversely affected by aspirin. Therefore, pregnant women and nursing mothers must treat aspirin as if it were a prescription drug—to be avoided unless a physician says otherwise. In coming years this prohibition may be considered unnecessary, but until more research is completed we prefer to err on the side of caution.

KIDNEY AND LIVER PROBLEMS

People who suffer from liver or kidney ailments must be very cautious no matter what pain reliever they use. Aspirin, acetaminophen, and ibuprofen can all be hard on these crucial organs. No one should take aspirin on a regular basis without very careful medical monitoring.

ULCERS

The most common side effects of aspirin involve the digestive tract—stomach upset, indigestion, heartburn, and nausea. Ulcers are common with regular aspirin use, even when it is taken in relatively low doses. Anyone with a history of perforated or bleeding ulcers must never take aspirin without medical supervision.

Although a doctor may be monitoring you carefully, it is not always possible to tell what kind of damage is being done to your stomach lining. Vigilance is critical. Report any symptoms of distress immediately. That includes frequent heartburn or indigestion. If you develop a full feeling before you have eaten your normal amount at mealtime, that could be an indication of trouble. If you find that you are losing weight without working at it, call the doctor's office promptly. And if you find that you feel under the weather or fatigued, go in for a checkup.

MISCELLANEOUS

❑ **Watch out for ringing in the ears.** People with this problem (tinnitus) could be experiencing an aspirin overdose. One of the first signs of trouble is a ringing sound, difficulty hearing, or other hearing disturbance. Check in with an ear, nose, and throat specialist if the sound doesn't go away with reduced aspirin doses.

❑ **People with gout or anemia** should take aspirin only under a doctor's supervision. Both conditions can be aggravated by aspirin. Interestingly, large doses of aspirin may actually improve gout, but this is not a do-it-yourself project.

❑ **Beware drug interactions.** Many prescription medicines can cause complications when they are combined with aspirin. In some situations aspirin can be lethal in the wrong combination. Anyone taking *any* other medicine—especially those listed in Appendix III—should consult a pharmacist or physician.

Even healthy individuals should periodically check in with a doctor if they are planning to take low-dose aspirin for prolonged periods of time. Aspirin is a wonder drug, but like any medicine it must be treated with respect!

References

1. Fields, W.S., et al. "Controlled Trial of Aspirin in Cerebral Ischemia." *Stroke* 1977; 8:301–316.
2. The Canadian Cooperative Study Group. "A Randomized Trial of Aspirin and Sulfinpyrazone in Threatened Stroke." *N. Engl. J. Med.* 1987; 299:53–59.
3. The ESPS Group. "The European Stroke Prevention Study (ESPS): Principal End-Points." *Lancet* 1987; 2:1351–1354.
4. UK-TIA Study Group. "United Kingdom Transient Ischemic Attack (UK-TIA) Aspirin Trial: Interim Results." *Br. Med. J.* 1988; 296:316–320.
5. Petersen, P., et al. "Placebo-Controlled, Randomised Trial of Warfarin and Aspirin for Prevention of Thromboembolic Complications in Chronic Atrial Fibrillation: The Copenhagen AFASAK Study." *Lancet* 1989; 1:175–179.
6. Stroke Prevention in Atrial Fibrillation Study Group Investigators. "Preliminary Report of the Stroke Prevention in Atrial Fibrillation Study." *N. Engl. J. Med.* 1990; 322:863–868.
7. The Dutch TIA Trial Study Group. "A Comparison of Two Doses of Aspirin (30 mg vs. 283 mg a Day) in Patients After a Transient Ischemic Attack or Minor Ischemic Stroke." *N. Engl. J. Med.* 1991; 325:1261–1266.
8. Ibid.
9. Olin, Bernie R., ed. *Drug Facts and Comparisons*, 1992 ed. St. Louis: Facts and Comparisons (A Wolters Kluwer Company), 1992.
10. Sherman, David G., et al. "Antithrombotic Therapy for Cerebrovascular Disorders (Third ACCP Concensus Conference on Antithrombotic Therapy)." *Chest* 1992; 102:529S–538S
11. The Steering Committee of the Physicians' Health Study

Research Group. "Special Report: Preliminary Report: Findings From the Aspirin Component of the Ongoing Physicians' Health Study." *N. Engl. J. Med.* 1988; 318:262–264.

12. Steering Committee of the Physicians' Health Study Research Group. "Final Report on the Aspirin Component of the Ongoing Physicians' Health Study." *N. Engl. J. Med.* 1989; 321:129–135.

13. Mayo, Nancy E., et al. "Aspirin and Hemorrhagic Stroke." *Stroke* 1991; 22:1213–1214.

14. ISIS-2 Collaborative Group. "Randomised Trial of Intravenous Streptokinase, Oral Aspirin, Both, or Neither Among 17,187 Cases of Suspected Acute Myocardial Infarction: ISIS-2." *Lancet* 1988; 2:349–360.

15. Stroke Prevention in Atrial Fibrillation Study Group Investigators, op. cit.

16. Barnett, H.J.M. "Drug Treatment of Stroke and Ischemic Brain: From Acetylsalicylic Acid to New Drugs— 100 Years of Pharmacology at Bayer Wuppertal-Eilberfeld: Aspirin in Stroke Prevention: An Overview." *Stroke* 1990; 21(12S):IV40–IV43.

17. Davis, Devra Lee, and Buffler, Patricia. "Reduction of Deaths After Drug Labelling for Risk of Reye's Syndrome." *Lancet* 1992; 340:1042.

18. The DAMAD Study Group. "Effect of Aspirin Alone and Aspirin Plus Dipyridamole in Early Diabetic Retinopathy: A Multicenter Randomized Controlled Clinical Trial." *Diabetes* 1989; 38:491–498.

THE BENEFITS OF ASPIRIN

CHAPTER 4

USING ASPIRIN TO TREAT AND PREVENT HEADACHES

Every day Americans swallow 80 million aspirin tablets. Much of that aspirin goes for headache relief. At roughly half a penny per pill, nothing else comes close in value. Generic ibuprofen or acetaminophen can cost five to ten times as much.

❏ **How good *is* aspirin?** For garden variety headaches, you can't beat it. Most people find that within half an hour of popping two pills headache pain is starting to go away. After an hour the pain is completely gone.

❏ **Watch out for headache rebound!** There is one very important caution, however. As good as aspirin can be against headaches, it should not be taken daily. Although arthritis victims can take regular doses of aspirin to relieve pain and inflammation, headache sufferers should not follow in their footsteps. Dr. Joel Saper is founder and director of the Michigan Head-Pain and Neurological Institute. He is one of the counry's leading headache authorities. Dr. Saper recommends that in general "analgesics should not be used more than two days per week, and more ideally less often, due to 'rebound phenomenon.' "[1]

This means that pain becomes worse as the medicine wears off. Dr. Saper has found that overusing nonprescription headache remedies (whether they contain aspirin, ibuprofen, or acetaminophen) can lead to the "vicious cycle syndrome," in which people keep using headache pills to relieve the pain that the drugs have created. Dr. Saper has seen some patients who take a fistfull of pills every day and still can't get relief from their chronic headaches.

❏ **Caffeine and aspirin.** One of the most controversial analgesic combinations on pharmacy shelves involves caffeine. For years **APC** tablets (aspirin, phenacetin, and caffeine) were a staple in the military for headaches and other pain. When phenacetin was found to increase the risk of kidney damage, it was removed from all over-the-counter products. Caffeine still remains, though, in products such as **Anacin, Excedrin**, and **Vanquish**. Prescription pain relievers that include caffeine in their formulations include **Cafergot, Darvon Compound-65, Fioricet, Fiorinal, Norgesic, Synalgos-DC**, and **Wigraine**.

According to Dr. Saper, "Some reports suggest that caffeine improves pain relief, exerts a favorable influence on mood, and enhances intestinal absorption of ergotamine [a migraine medicine] and other substances. Other studies do not substantiate these claims."[2] What we do know is that modest amounts of caffeine (as little as 100 mg) on a regular basis can produce a withdrawal syndrome characterized by "headache, drowsiness, fatigue, decreased performance, and in some instances, nausea and vomiting."[3,4]

An elegant study published in the *New England Journal of Medicine* confirms that when caffeine is discontinued, it can precipitate moderate or severe headaches.[5] The investigators found that this effect occurred with the amount of caffeine found in two and a half cups of coffee or the amount that might easily be consumed from caffeine-containing analgesics in a day. The moral of this story is that even if caffeine can enhance the pain-relieving effect of aspirin, you should limit the use of such medications to two days a week. Otherwise you may be courting the vicious cycle syndrome.

❑   ❑   ❑   ❑

Q. I take a couple of aspirin for a headache once or twice a month. My husband takes three aspirin instead of two for similar symptoms. Is he getting any more relief than I am? Should I consider taking more?

A. Probably not. Aspirin has been proven effective against a wide variety of headaches (garden variety, tension, some migraines) in standard doses. Dr. Seymour Diamond, one of the country's leading headache experts, cites studies that compared two regular-strength aspirin tablets (650 mg) against three regular-strength acetaminophen tablets (1,000 mg) and two to four ibuprofen tablets (400 mg to 800 mg). The standard aspirin dose was comparable to the other pain relievers when it came to relieving tension headaches.

Our suggestion would be to use the lowest effective dose that works for you. There is no need to go to three tablets if two will do the trick. Your husband may have convinced himself that more is better, but we doubt that the extra tablet is providing any additional headache relief.

Q. I get migraine headaches and need help. How can I use aspirin to prevent them?

A. The Physicians' Health Study reported a 20 percent reduction in migraines when the doctors took one regular-strength (325 mg) aspirin tablet every other day.[6] A British study produced even better results.[7] The physician-subjects had 30 percent fewer migraines, prompting the lead investigator, Dr. Richard Peto, to suggest "a migraine patient should consider taking a baby aspirin a day."[8] This is strictly in the interest of prevention, as the 81 mg in a baby aspirin is too little to treat any adult's headache.

When it comes to migraine treatment, you should always check with your physician first. There have been a number of new developments in the treatment of this devastating condition. The most exciting advance is the drug **Imitrex** (sumatriptan). This prescription medicine can take away most migraines within one hour. The biggest downside, however, is the cost. Compared to aspirin, **Imitrex** is unbelievably expensive.

Q. How does aspirin prevent migraines?

A. No one really knows. It is clearly a different mechanism from the one that provides standard headache relief. Remember, we're talking about very low doses of aspirin (one tablet every other day or even as little as a baby aspirin). You couldn't even relieve a normal headache with that dose.

Severe migraines are to headaches what Moby Dick was to a minnow. Scientists speculate that aspirin may keep platelets from clumping. This may in turn diminish the release of serotonin in the brain. This neurochemical is thought to play a critical role in migraine headaches.

Q. Why is it that aspirin is *so* great for relieving my muscular aches and pains, but it doesn't do a thing for my headaches?

A. People vary widely in their response to aspirin for various ailments. Aspirin appears to work through a different mechanism for headache pain than for muscle pain. Some people appear to get more headache relief from ibuprofen (**Advil, Motrin IB, Nuprin**, etc.). If ibuprofen does no better than aspirin, you might try acetaminophen.

Q. I have premenstrual migraines three to five days per month. They are so bad I can't stand to blink my eyes or to touch a hair on my head. So I am very interested in

learning more about the unexpected finding that one aspirin every other day can reduce migraines.

A. Menstrual migraines turn out to be a lot more common than most people would imagine. One approach is to take an anti-inflammatory drug (preferably ibuprofen—**Advil, Motrin IB, Nuprin**, etc.), starting roughly one week before your period. Precise dose is hard to ascertain for any given individual, so you may have to experiment, starting with the lowest dose (one or two 200-mg tablets daily) to see if it is effective.

Another option is to use an estrogen-containing prescription medication. Many British clinicians suggest using an estrogen patch (such as **Estraderm**) starting the week before menstruation.

We hasten to note that most current studies that suggest that aspirin is beneficial in preventing migraines were carried out in men. One out of five migraine victims found that one aspirin tablet every other day appeared to lessen their attacks. We don't have any evidence to suggest that aspirin will do the same for women who suffer severe headaches around the time of their periods.

❑   ❑   ❑   ❑

References

1. Saper, Joel R., et al. *Handbook of Headache Management: A Practical Guide to Diagnosis and Treatment of Head, Neck, and Facial Pain.* Baltimore: Williams & Wilkins, 1993, p. 37.
2. Saper, Joel R. *Help for Headaches.* New York: Warner Books, 1987, p. 213.
3. Hughes, John R. "Clinical Importance of Caffeine Withdrawal." *N. Engl. J. Med.* 1992; 327:1160–1161.
4. Griffiths, R.R., et al. "Caffeine Physical Dependence: A Re-

view of Human and Laboratory Animal Studies.'' *Psychopharmacology* 1988; 94:437–451.

5. Silverman, Kenneth, et al. ''Withdrawal Syndrome After the Double-Blind Cessation of Caffeine Consumption.'' *N. Engl. J. Med.* 1992; 327:1109–1114.

6. Buring, Julie E., et al. ''Low-Dose Aspirin for Migraine Prophylaxis.'' *JAMA* 1990; 264:1711–1713.

7. Peto, R., et al. ''Randomised Trial of Prophylactic Daily Aspirin in British Male Doctors.'' *Br. Med. J.* 1988; 296:313–316.

8. Peto, R. ''Treating Migraine.'' *Br. Med. J.* 1989; 299:517.

CHAPTER 5

USING ASPIRIN FOR EXERCISE INJURIES

Half-empty aspirin bottles are a common sight in most gyms and athletic training facilities. Long before there was **Advil** or even **Tylenol**, athletes were using aspirin to ease their sprains, strains, and sore muscles. The analgesic effect provides immediate benefit and the anti-inflammatory action offers added relief. Our favorite wonder drug turns out to be a powerful aid for the pain of exercise injuries or overworked muscles.

❑ ❑ ❑ ❑

Q. I am a competitive runner and frequently take aspirin after a race or long training run. What is the proper dose for sprains and other exercise injuries? Would ibuprofen be better?

A. For typical muscle strains and other soft tissue injuries, the standard dose is two to three aspirin tablets (650 to 975 mg) every four hours. This will provide analgesic action (pain relief) and also help control the inflammation. There is no good data that larger doses (three or four regular-strength tablets) will provide any additional benefits.

Within 30 minutes of taking aspirin, blood salicylate levels should be adequate to start providing benefit. Maximum effect is achieved within two hours and gradually diminishes over the next several hours. Food will slow the whole process down; how much depends on the nature of the meal.

Ibuprofen (**Advil, Motrin IB, Nuprin**, etc.) will also work for the injuries you describe. A standard dose would be 200 to 400 mg (one to two tablets) every four to six hours (not to exceed six tablets in 24 hours unless under medical supervision). We cannot say that it will be noticeably more effective than aspirin, though. As a long-distance runner, you have had to learn to listen to your body. We suggest you try one analgesic one time and then compare the relief against the other analgesic the next. Go with whichever seems most effective.

Q. What are the best guidelines for using aspirin to treat tendinitis?

A. Tendinitis (inflammation of the tendon) can be extremely painful. We know from personal experience the agony of tennis elbow. Repetitive trauma or unaccustomed exercise is frequently responsible for this condition. Such damage should respond to aspirin as would any soft-tissue injury or inflammation. Two or three tablets (650 to 975 mg) every four hours is a standard dose. If the injury is severe, however, it is possible that additional pain relief with a prescription analgesic will be necessary to supplement the aspirin.

Immobilize the painful area if at all possible. Don't be a dummy and continue to play tennis (as we have been known to do) and then expect the injury to improve. Heat or cold (depending on which feels best) can also be beneficial.

Q. Some football coaches reportedly tell their players to take six aspirin after a hard game to help healing as well as provide pain relief. Is this advisable? If so, should they take it before or after the game?

A. We are unaware of any evidence that aspirin can speed healing of traumatized tissues. But it can certainly reduce inflammation and ease pain. We would be very cautious about encouraging football players to take so much aspirin before a game. The anticlotting effects might lead to increased bruising and bleeding from all the blocking and tackling. Even after a game, six tablets all at once could cause some players problems.

Q. I had suffered from lower back pain and other muscular aches after gardening for years. Then my doctor suggested that I take two aspirin *before* I went out to the garden. This has worked like magic. I never realized that aspirin could be used to prevent as well as treat these kinds of aches and pains.

A. Tennis players, runners, and other athletes have long reported that sometimes a little preventive medicine can be very useful in heading off serious pain later on. This may be because we now know aspirin works both at the site of inflammation (in tennis elbow, for example) and in the spinal cord to calm down pain sensations. By preventing activation of those nerves ahead of time, the level of pain may be substantially diminished.

Ibuprofen also should be effective for this purpose. Researchers in the field of sports medicine have shown that pre-treating with ibuprofen can delay the onset of muscle soreness and help restore function. It cannot, however, prevent damage to an overworked muscle. We know several physicians who take ibuprofen about half an hour before hitting the tennis ball to diminish the inflammation associated with tennis elbow. They would probably be better advised to build up their muscles with special exercises and to wear a special strap that takes the pressure off their tender tendon.

❑   ❑   ❑   ❑

CHAPTER 6

ASPIRIN FOR ARTHRITIS, RHEUMATISM, AND INFLAMMATION

Willow bark has been used for ages to relieve pain and inflammation. A Greek physician, Dioscorides, probably prescribed it in the first century to patients with rheumatism. No doubt Native American healers also used it for this purpose long before Columbus landed.

In 1828 a German pharmacologist isolated the active ingredient, salicin, from willow bark, and in 1838 it was given the name we know today—salicylic acid. By the mid 1850s Germany dominated the willow bark business. But natural forms of aspirin were tough on the tummy. "Users of the time compared them to having fire ants in the stomach."[1]

Soon synthetic variations became available. By 1877 British, German, and French physicians had reported treatment success for rheumatic fever, rheumatoid arthritis, and gout. Unfortunately, these salicylate derivatives were also hard on the digestive tract. Dr. Felix Hoffman, a German chemist charged with developing dye for the Bayer company, began searching for something better. His arthritic father was taking sodium salicylate and complaining bitterly of stomach pains. In 1898 Dr. Hoffman's father became a guinea pig for acetylsalicylic acid and found that it was more effective for his arthritis and more palatable.[2] On March 6, 1899, the official trade name Aspirin was granted to Bayer AG.

Aspirin has been a mainstay in the treatment of arthritis ever since. And no wonder. Aspirin offers a nice one-two punch against arthritis: (1) It directly affects the level of pain and inflammation in sore joints and tissues; (2) it also relieves pain at the level of the spinal cord where the pain sensations are normally amplified and relayed to the brain.

What most people don't realize is that there are two distinct dosing programs for arthritis and other inflammatory disorders. When used without a prescription, the maximum total 24-hour dosage of aspirin is 4,000 mg (12 regular-strength tablets). That is enough to provide substantial pain relief and perhaps even some anti-inflammatory action.

To really achieve noticeable anti-inflammatory improvements in rheumatoid arthritis, doctors often prescribe 4,000 to 6,000 mg daily (12 to 18 regular-strength aspirin tablets). This is clearly not a self-directed treatment program. Anyone who takes large doses of aspirin must be under the care and supervision of a knowledgeable physician.

How does aspirin compare to other arthritis medicine? That is a much harder question to answer than you might think. There is an overabundance of anti-inflammatory drugs (NSAIDs) on the market. Most are available only by prescription, but ibuprofen (**Advil, Bayer Select Pain Relief, Excedrin IB, Midol IB, Motrin IB, Nuprin**, etc.) has proved to be a very popular over-the-counter pain reliever and naproxen (**Anaprox** and **Naprosyn**) may also become available without prescription. Prescription NSAIDs include **Ansaid, Clinoril, Dolobid, Feldene, Indocin, Lodine, Meclomen, Motrin, Nalfon, Orudis, Relafen, Tolectin**, and **Voltaren**.

There have been few well-designed studies that fairly compare anti-inflammatory doses of aspirin with other NSAIDs, so it is hard to say that one drug is superior to or safer than another. Some rheumatologists we know have come to the conclusion that all these drugs are roughly comparable. Some last a relatively short period of time and, like aspirin, must be taken three or four times a day. Others, such as **Feldene** or **Relafen**, are so long-acting that one daily dose suffices. This convenience does not mean these once-a-day drugs are more effective than aspirin.

Whenever a new NSAID hits the market, there is initial enthusiasm which usually wanes over time. People discover that the benefits are not noticeably greater than those they experience with older medications and side effects are comparable. At anti-inflammatory doses aspirin provides similar pain relief at a fraction of the cost. It may be more irritating to the stomach, but all the NSAIDs can cause bleeding, ulcers, and perforations of the digestive tract.

It doesn't matter whether you are treating arthritis, tendinitis, bursitis, or a bad back. All the NSAIDs work through the same pathway to reduce inflammation, swelling, and pain. Some people may respond better to one than another, so you and your doctor may have to experiment a bit to find the best one for you. Careful monitoring is essential, whether you take aspirin, ibuprofen, or a pricey prescription NSAID.

❑   ❑   ❑   ❑

Q. I am on my feet all day long. By the end of the day my hips and legs bother me something terrible. I have tried various pills the doctors suggest, but have found that nothing works half as well as aspirin. I always get relief within half an hour.

A. This reaction to aspirin sounds almost as if it came right out of the textbook. Salicylate levels reach a therapeutic level within 30 minutes. Pain from degenerative arthritis or osteoarthritis should start easing as salicylate levels climb. Aspirin will provide both pain relief and anti-inflammatory action.

Q. I was astonished to see my aunt swallow four aspirin tablets at lunch the other day. She says her doctor told her to take that many four times a day for severe arthritis. Isn't that overkill? I take aspirin for stiff fingers, but I only need a couple of pills every six hours. Why is she taking so much?

A. It sounds like your aunt suffers from rheumatoid arthritis. This condition is thought to be an autoimmune disease. The body begins attacking itself almost as if joints and cartilage were foreign invaders. The resulting inflammation and pain can be crippling. To calm the storm, physicians may recommend anywhere from 12 to 18 regular-strength aspirin tablets daily—sometimes even more. Some doctors will increase the dose to a near-toxic level, stopping only when the patient begins experiencing a ringing in the ears (tinnitus). They will then back down from that peak to a level at which the ringing in the ears disappears.

When people take 4,000 to 6,000 mg of aspirin daily, the effects are profound. At that level aspirin has both anti-inflammatory actions and immune-modulating effects. White blood cells (the body's shock troops against infection) are less likely to attach themselves to joint tissues and produce irritation. Aspirin may also work in part to alter connective tissue composition, so joints and cartilage are less prone to destruction.

Such high doses of aspirin can lead to serious complications. Indigestion, heartburn, stomach bleeding and ulceration are common. Ringing in the ears is a very real danger and represents an early warning sign of damage to the ears. Liver damage can also occur and periodic blood tests are essential to rule out this complication. Signs of aspirin overdose include dizziness, impaired hearing, headache, confusion, nausea, vomiting, sweating, and drowsiness. Obviously, your aunt's doctor must monitor her situation very carefully to make sure she doesn't get into trouble.

Your situation sounds quite different. Stiff fingers, knees, shoulders, and hips can be signs of osteoarthritis, the normal wear and tear associated with accumulating lots of birthdays. For this kind of arthritis, regular aspirin doses work primarily to relieve pain, just as acetaminophen (**Anacin-3, Panadol, Tylenol**, etc.) does. The usual recommendation is two tablets every four hours.

Q. Is aspirin useful in treating the pain of osteoporosis? Can it be taken safely for this condition? If so, what is the recommended dose?

A. Osteoporosis does not normally cause pain unless there are small fractures of the spine or unless someone falls and breaks a bone. Aspirin will provide some degree of analgesia for any break, but it may not be strong enough to provide enough benefit for serious pain.

Q. I take high doses of aspirin for my arthritis and I don't like taking so many pills all the time. I always feel like they are going to get stuck in my throat. Are there some safe forms of aspirin that provide more than the regular dose?

A. You're in luck! A number of safe and effective preparations come in higher doses. A few examples: **Ascriptin Extra Strength** (500 mg), **Alka-Seltzer Extra Strength** (500 mg), **Maximum Bayer** (500 mg), **Maximum Strength Ecotrin** (500 mg), **Extra Strength Bufferin** (500 mg), **A.S.A. Enseals** (650 mg), **Arthritis Strength BC Powder** (742 mg), and prescription-strength **Easprin** (975 mg). (See Chapter 17 for further details.)

Q. My doctor suggested that I should take one baby aspirin daily to prevent blood clots. Will I still get the heart attack prevention benefits of aspirin if I take larger daily doses for my arthritis?

A. This is an incredibly sophisticated question. Most Americans subscribe to the "more is better" theory. That is why we have extra-strength, adult-strength, and arthritis-strength pain relievers. Regular-strength seems so wimpy. But when it comes to heart attack prevention, less may be best.

First, let us say that there has never been a large-scale study that compared mini aspirin doses (like the 81 mg in baby aspirin) to large doses used for arthritis. We are probably years away from having a true answer to this question. Although large daily doses of aspirin will reduce the risk of blood clots and probably afford substantial protection against heart attacks, there is some doubt that such amounts are optimal. (They certainly carry greater risks.) The reason is that when you take more than a single tablet of aspirin, you eliminate a natural substance that can protect against vasoconstriction and clotting. That compound is prostacyclin, and it seems to act as the body's own clot preventer. Preliminary data suggest that small aspirin doses may be more effective than one regular-strength tablet when it comes to clot pre-vention.[3]

This does not mean you have to give up taking aspirin for arthritis. We encourage you to discuss this fascinating issue with your cardiologist. You are probably getting significant protection, but perhaps not quite as much as you would if you stuck to the mini-doses.

Q. I have been taking high-dose aspirin for over five years, but lately I don't seem to get the relief for my arthritis I used to. Could I have built up a resistance to aspirin? Should I increase my dose?

A. The textbooks tell us that people are not supposed to build up resistance or develop tolerance to aspirin or other anti-inflammatory drugs like ibuprofen (**Advil, Motrin IB, Nuprin,** etc.). You are not the first person, though, to say that after a while relief appears to fade. If this effect exists, it is clearly different from the rapid tolerance that develops with narcotic pain relievers like codeine (**Tylenol** Nos. 2, 3, and 4 or **Empirin** Nos. 2, 3, and 4), hydrocodone

(**Anexsia 5, Lorcet-HD, Lortab 5, Vicodin**) or oxycodone (**Percocet, Tylox, Percodan**) or propoxyphene (**Darvocet-N** and **Darvon**).

We would advise against increasing the aspirin dose to try to achieve your previous level of pain relief. First, there are no data to suggest that doing so would work, and there is reason to believe you would increase your risk of side effects. An alternative solution might be to take a "drug holiday" from aspirin. Check with your doctor to see what he might recommend as an alternate analgesic for a while. When you come back to aspirin, you may find it will work as well as it once did.

❑ ❑ ❑ ❑

References

1. Dolan, Carrie. "What Soothes Aches, Makes Flowers Last, And Grows Hair?" *Wall Street Journal*, Feb. 19, 1988, p. 1.
2. Weissmann, Gerald. "Aspirin." *Scientific American* 1991; 264:84–90.
3. Fiore, Louis D., et al. "The Bleeding Time Response to Aspirin." *Am. J. Clin. Pathol.* 1990; 94:292–296.

CHAPTER 7

USING ASPIRIN TO TREAT A FEVER

Native healers used willow bark for centuries to bring down fevers, but it wasn't until 1763 that Western medicine tried it. That was when the Reverend Edmund Stone of Oxfordshire, England, noted that bark of the willow tree was good for the "agues." These fevers or chills were associated with swampy areas where the English willow grew. In his simple-minded way, the Reverend Stone apparently figured that the cure might also be found in close proximity to the place where people suffered the most from swamp fever. He tried chewing the bark and *voila,* he noted improvement. (Actually, six years of careful observation went into his discovery.) His successful experiment was reported to the president of the Royal Society. The rest is history. There is still no better medicine than aspirin to bring down a fever.

❑   ❑   ❑   ❑

Q. When should you treat a fever with aspirin? I thought a fever was supposed to be a part of the natural healing process. Wouldn't aspirin just get in the way?

A. A very perceptive question. While you are quite right that an elevated temperature may be beneficial for the healing process, a fever can make you feel awful. Many people find that they can rest more comfortably if their temperature comes down. And if the temperature is really elevated—say around 103 to 105 degrees—then you almost certainly will want to knock it down to prevent neurological injury from the high temperature. In fact, at that level you should be under medical care anyway.

Q. Is Tylenol just as good as aspirin for bringing down a fever?

A. Acetaminophen (**Anacin-3, APAP, Panadol, Tylenol,** etc.), aspirin, and ibuprofen (**Advil, Motrin IB, Nuprin,** etc.) are all roughly comparable when it comes to controlling fever.

Because of the fear of Reye's syndrome, aspirin has fallen out of favor for children and teenagers, especially if it is uncertain what the cause of the fever may be. In the early stages flu and chicken pox are sometimes hard to distinguish from a garden variety cold. Acetaminophen and ibuprofen are available in children's doses and are preferable if the cause of the fever is uncertain.

Q. Perhaps you could help a confused parent: How much aspirin should I give my three children? (One is 12, one is 3, and one is just a baby.) I have received recommendations of very different doses from different doctors.

A. You are not alone in your confusion. While the adult aspirin dose is easy to remember—one or two tablets every four hours—the children's dose is far more complicated.

Even the official guidelines in the medical literature read like so much medical mumbo jumbo: 65 mg/kg/24 hours in four to six divided doses. The maximum daily dose should never exceed 3,600 mg. To actually figure out what a particular child should take at any given time would require a conversion table (kg to pounds) and a calculator to compute.

To prove how complex this issue is, several pediatricians mailed a questionnaire to roughly 6,000 of their colleagues.

Of the 2,296 physicians who answered the questions, the variability in prescribing patterns was mind-boggling.[1] Some pediatricians recommended aspirin every three hours while others preferred every four to six hours. Dosage also varied. There were doctors who prescribed based on age— some suggested 65 mg for each year, while others believed 81 mg was right for each year of age. Many of the doctors recommended parents use weight as a guideline—one baby aspirin for each 10 to 15 pounds of body weight. A significant minority believed a higher dose was appropriate.

These pediatricians offered a simpler formula than the official version and we have tried to make it even more practical. Our conclusion is that one baby aspirin (81 mg) for each 12 pounds of body weight is about as close as you can get. That means if your child weighs 24 pounds, she should receive two baby aspirins; 36 pounds equals three tablets and 48 pounds equals four tablets. If a child weighs an uneven amount (almost guaranteed in real life), just divide the weight by 12. In other words, if Suzy weighs 30 pounds, divide by 12, and you get two and a half baby aspirin tablets every 3 to 4 hours. A child who weighs 48 pounds or more, is at least 6 years old, and can swallow regular tablets may be given a single standard 325-mg aspirin tablet in place of four baby aspirin tablets, if it is more convenient.

Because of the very real fear of Reye's syndrome, however, we always recommend that parents contact their family physician or pediatrician before administering aspirin to children or teenagers.

Q. Why does aspirin lower a fever but won't reduce normal body temperature?

A. Body temperature is incredibly complicated. It can be modified by hormones, exercise, heat, and of course infection. The hypothalamus is a specialized structure within the brain that is thought to play a crucial role in temperature regulation. When the body is invaded by viruses or bacteria, an immunological response is mobilized which in turn causes the hypothalamus to elevate the set point. This natural thermostat is affected by hormonelike chemicals called prostaglandins. Since aspirin helps block the production of prostaglandins in the area of the hypothalamus, the set point comes down and the thermostat brings the temperature down.[2] The effect is only temporary, though. As the effect of aspirin wears off and prostaglandin levels climb, the set point is elevated and temperature goes back up.

When body temperature is normal, there are no unusual prostaglandins in the area of the brain responsible for altering the thermostat. Consequently, aspirin has no effect on the set point and temperature doesn't change.

❑   ❑   ❑   ❑

References

1. Done, Alan K., et al. "Aspirin Dosage for Infants." *J. of Ped.* 1979; 95:617–624.
2. Gilman, Alfred G., et al., eds. *Goodman and Gilman's The Pharmacological Basis of Therapeutics,* 8th ed. New York: Pergamon Press, 1990, p. 641.

CHAPTER 8

USING ASPIRIN TO HELP PREVENT HEART ATTACK, STROKE, AND BLOOD CLOTS

Five million Americans have clogged coronary arteries. Each year there are 1.25 million heart attacks in the United States.[1] Over 600,000 people die, either from coronary attacks or complications of heart disease.[2] Half a million more suffer strokes annually.[3] Many don't survive. Hundreds of thousands of others are left with debilitating paralysis and impairment that forever alters the quality of their lives. Cardiovascular catastrophes are by far our number one killer.

That's the bad news. But the good news is that the numbers keep looking better and better all the time. Over the last 30 years the incidence of coronary heart disease has dropped by an extraordinary 50 percent.[4] The reduction in stroke mortality (more than 6 percent per year) has been even more impressive.[5]

Success has many fathers. Such fabulous improvement over the last few decades has been attributed to better diet and lower cholesterol, use of blood pressure medicines, increased exercise, consumption of vitamins, and improved medical care. Drug companies have been especially quick to take credit for the drop in deaths from strokes and heart attacks. The problem is that no large-scale study has been able to show that cholesterol-lowering medicines actually improve overall mortality. Even more surprising, the same is true for blood pressure-lowering drugs. Use of such medications doesn't always seem to correlate well with a reduction in deaths from heart attacks or strokes.[6,7] The declines in both strokes and coronary heart problems actually started well before the big campaign to control hypertension.[8]

One possible explanation for the great improvement of the last 30 years has been mostly overlooked—aspirin. Dr. Lewis Thomas is one of America's greatest physicians, educators, administrators, and philosophers. He has been dean of the School of Medicine at Yale University and of New York University School of Medicine. He was president and chief executive officer of Memorial Sloan-Kettering Cancer Center. He has been a professor of medicine, pediatrics, and pathology at many other prestigious institutions.

But Dr. Thomas is probably best known by the public for his wonderful books, *The Lives of a Cell* and *The Medusa and the Snail*. His most recent work is *The Fragile Species* (Charles Scribner's Sons, 1992). He offers the following explanation for the cardiovascular gains we have seen in this country: "My own theory is that the 20 percent drop in American coronary disease was the result of commercial television, which appeared in the early 1950's and has made a substantial part of its living ever since through the incessant advertising, all day and all night, of household remedies for headache and back pain, all containing aspirin."

Could it be that the lowly aspirin is really responsible for the astounding drop in heart attacks and strokes? We may never know for sure, but one thing seems certain. In study after study, aspirin use reduces death rate anywhere from 20 to 50 percent—comparable to the overall reductions we have seen nationwide in strokes and heart attacks.

THE CAUSES OF HEART ATTACK AND STROKE

Cardiologists and neurologists are still arguing about what actually causes cardiovascular accidents—heart attacks and strokes. One theory has it that there is a sudden spasm in an artery—like pinching a straw while you are trying to drink. Strong emotions or intense exercise can release adrenaline (the fight-or-flight hormone), which can produce such a spasm. The spasm can in turn cut off blood flow to the heart or brain, leading to a heart attack or stroke.

An alternate view is that atherosclerotic plaque (composed of cholesterol, calcium, and other material) that has built up in arteries predisposes to blood clots. When the plaque cracks or fractures, platelets (the sticky part of blood) rush to the area and begin to form a blood clot. As the clot enlarges, it restricts blood flow and oxygen delivery to the surrounding tissue. Damage occurs and part of the heart or brain dies. During a heart attack irregular heart rhythms (arrhythmias) can result, and they sometimes cause sudden death.

Thrombotic strokes can also happen when a blood clot that originates somewhere else in the body is carried to the brain. People who experience atrial fibrillation (a strange, irregular rhythm in the upper chamber of the heart that can go undetected) often have such clots. For such individuals, strokes caused by clots are a major risk. (Hemorrhagic strokes, on the other hand, are caused by blood leaking from the vessels into the brain where it causes damage directly. This type of stroke is less common but equally serious. Aspirin can't prevent this hazard.)

The beauty of very low dose aspirin is that it may be beneficial regardless of whether a blood clot or a vessel spasm is the bad actor. To understand why you have to know about two natural chemicals—thromboxane A_2 and prostacyclin. Thromboxane is a bad guy—think of it as a traitor to the body because it makes blood platelets stickier and therefore more likely to come together to form a clot. It also can cause blood vessels to constrict—just like squeezing a straw to restrict passage of a liquid.

Prostacyclin, on the other hand, provides an opposite effect. Not only does it prevent platelet stickiness, it also has a dilating action. In other words, prostacyclin appears naturally helpful in preventing the condition that could lead to heart attacks and strokes.

Researchers have assumed that increasing prostacyclin and reducing thromboxane A_2 should be beneficial. Unfortunately, at standard doses aspirin halts the body's ability to make both thromboxane and prostacyclin. At small doses, though, about 30 to 75 mg daily, the body's thromboxane output is diminished, while its prostacyclin production is unaffected. European research confirms that 30 mg works in practice as well as in theory, and may be just as effective in preventing minor strokes (transient ischemic attacks, or TIAs for short) as bigger doses. Presumably, such a small dose is less likely to cause side effects.[9]

Transient Ischemic Attacks (TIAs)

People often pass off their little "spells" as stress-related incidents. Temporary symptoms may include blindness in one eye, numbness or tingling accompanied by paralysis on one side of the body, weakness, inability to talk, confusion, or dizziness. These attacks can last anywhere from a few minutes to a couple of hours. Because people usually recover completely, they may disregard this early warning sign of a possible future stroke. Anyone who has experienced something that could be a TIA should have a complete neurological workup.

THE IRON THEORY OF HEART ATTACK PREVENTION

An alternate, or perhaps supplemental, mechanism for aspirin's protective powers against heart attacks involves the controversial iron theory. Researchers have discovered that men with high iron levels in their blood have a substantially increased risk of heart attacks.[10] The "heart-iron" theory was first developed in 1981 when Dr. Jerome Sullivan was a resident physician in Tampa, Florida. He was unhappy with the usual explanation as to why middle-aged women were far less likely to experience heart attacks than men.

Although most physicians attributed the difference to a protective effect of the female hormone estrogen, Dr. Sullivan looked for a different explanation. He came up with the novel idea that iron might be the key factor. Menstruating women lose blood each month and therefore tend to have lower iron levels. When women go through menopause and stop menstruating, their iron levels rise and so does their heart attack incidence. Dr. Sullivan speculated that increased blood iron levels might somehow promote atherosclerosis.[11]

Research has subsequently supported this extraordinary theory. People with high levels of iron (a condition called hemochromatosis) have an exceptionally high incidence of heart attacks early in life. Finnish researchers more recently found that even healthy men with "normal" iron levels (normal as defined by laboratory standards) have apparently double the risk of heart attack compared to men with slightly lower levels.[12]

Aspirin may in part help prevent heart attacks by lowering iron levels. Every time someone pops an aspirin tablet, even a small dose, the stomach bleeds. One could almost think of this as comparable to the monthly menstruation women go through—but at a microscopic level. Dr. Sullivan has speculated that this small regular bleeding process could keep iron levels lower and explain the protective effect of long-term use.[13]

Another possible explanation for aspirin's benefits may be its anti-oxidant activity. Highly reactive molecules called free radicals are thought to contribute to heart disease and atherosclerosis, not to mention generalized aging. Iron seems to promote the formation of free radicals. Anti-oxidants like vitamin C, vitamin E, beta carotene, and selenium are free radical scavengers. Aspirin might add to this protective effect. Whatever the ultimate mechanism proves to be, there is little doubt that tiny amounts of aspirin provide exceptional benefit.

❑   ❑   ❑   ❑

Q. Should I be taking aspirin to prevent a heart attack? My parents are alive and well in their seventies with no sign of heart problems. But my grandfather died of a heart attack and two uncles had heart attacks in their fifties. I used to smoke, but I quit eight years ago. If I ought to be taking aspirin, I don't have a clue to how much.

A. There is still no medical consensus on who should take aspirin to prevent a heart attack. However, people at highest risk would appear to be the leading candidates: especially those with unstable (hard to control) angina. If one believes the results of the Physicians' Health Study (involving 22,000 healthy male doctors), almost anyone moving into middle age might be a candidate for aspirin even if they are healthy (so long as they aren't allergic to aspirin, are not asthmatic, do not have a bleeding disorder, and do not have uncontrolled high blood pressure).

The proper dose is also still up for grabs. Clearly one regular-strength aspirin tablet every other day affords substantial benefit. But it is entirely possible that as little as one-half a baby aspirin tablet or one-eighth of a regular adult aspirin tablet (about 40 mg) daily may also provide substantial benefit—at considerably less risk. Since anyone who plans to take aspirin regularly for years (or decades) should be under medical supervision anyway, we recommend that you discuss appropriate doses with your physician.

Q. A friend told me that all the studies showing that aspirin helps prevent heart attacks and strokes were done *on men only!* Is there conclusive evidence that taking small daily doses of aspirin prevents these ailments in women as well?

A. You are quite right. Most of the studies on heart attack prevention *have* been done on men. That may seem rather sexist, and to a large degree it is. Researchers have traditionally focused their attention on men and ignored women in drug trials. There is another reason, however, and that is that women are far less likely than men to suffer heart attacks in middle age. Consequently, it is much more difficult—and more expensive—to organize studies that will produce meaningful results for women.

Part of the confusion stems from some early work carried out in Canada around 1970. The first placebo-controlled trial of aspirin against strokes demonstrated that four tablets daily lowered the risk of stroke and death from stroke by 48 percent . . . in men.[14] Women, who were included in the study, experienced no benefit whatsoever. But this may have been due to the fact that their numbers were so low. Only 179 women were included out of a total of 585 patients. A British study also showed that men were protected but women were not. Once again, however, they were underrepresented (only one fourth of total patients). These discouraging results led some investigators to speculate that women were different biologically and somehow could not benefit from aspirin.

Fortunately, subsequent studies, especially a large French investigation, have proven that notion wrong.[15] More good news comes from an especially well-designed research program developed to look specifically at women's health issues. Between 1980 and 1986, Harvard researchers followed 87,678 registered nurses. The researchers found that low-dose aspirin (one to six pills per week) lowered the women's risk of a first heart attack by roughly 30 percent.[16] This confirms that women are not much different from men when it comes to benefiting from aspirin.

These women took aspirin sporadically—one to six pills per week—for such symptoms as arthritis, sprains, strains, and headaches. Interestingly, women who took *more* than seven aspirin tablets per week did *not* show a cardioprotective effect. Further research on women is clearly needed to determine appropriate dose and extent of benefit. For now it appears that low-dose aspirin does help reduce the risk of a first heart attack in women and men alike.

Q. I have a history of strokes in my family. Any special guidelines for using aspirin to prevent my having one? Am I at greater risk?

A. There is substantial data to suggest that aspirin lowers the risk of stroke due to blood clots in the brain, but the story gets a bit complex. People who have had transient ischemic attacks (TIAs), a type of nondisabling mini-stroke, are at high risk of serious cardiovascular accidents and death. Studies have shown that doses ranging from one to five aspirin tablets daily can reduce the risk of such complications by 20 to 25 percent.[17] Many neurologists have recommended one regular-strength aspirin per day after a TIA or minor stroke.[18]

Newer research suggests that as little as 30 mg of aspirin (less than one tenth of a regular-strength tablet) may be just as effective in preventing vascular complications in people who have had TIAs or minor strokes.[19] Not surprisingly, such a low dose produced significantly fewer side effects than regular-strength aspirin. But the bottom line is that "the optimum dose [of aspirin] for stroke prevention remains unsettled."[20] We encourage you to discuss your risk factors with a physician who is up-to-date on the literature. Together you may be able to come to an agreement about the value of aspirin in your case and what the right dose should be if the decision is made to proceed.

Q. Does Naprosyn or any other prescription drug provide the same heart attack/stroke/migraine protection as aspirin? If not, can I take a small dose of aspirin daily, in addition to these drugs?

A. What a great question! Unfortunately, no studies have been done to help us determine the answer. At the moment, we simply do not know whether NSAIDs (nonsteroidal anti-inflammatory drugs) like **Naprosyn, Motrin, Feldene, Clinoril**, etc., reduce the risk of heart attacks or strokes.

We do know that adding aspirin to an NSAID may increase the risk of stomach irritation or ulceration. And some NSAIDs (**Nalfon** and **Indocin**, for example) may be partially inactivated by aspirin. A tiny aspirin dose (80 mg or less) might be worth the risk, but we would recommend embarking on such a course only after careful consultation with your physician.

Q. Isn't it more beneficial to take one half aspirin every day instead of one aspirin every second day?

A. The optimal aspirin dose and regimen for heart attack prevention has yet to be worked out. A decade ago most physicians had a hard time believing that one aspirin every other day would be very effective. Now we know that dose is quite good at preventing blood clots and heart attacks. New research will tell us what the best program is to achieve clear benefits with the fewest side effects.

Aspirin's anticlotting effects on platelets are surprisingly long lasting. One way to measure this impact is to calculate bleeding time. After a small incision the normal bleeding time in healthy men averages five minutes (under special test conditions).[21] Not surprisingly, aspirin prolongs bleeding time. The delay in clotting occurs within minutes and peaks between 4 and 12 hours after a single dose. Interestingly, this effect is the same whether you take a baby aspirin or a regular-strength (325 mg) tablet.[22] The increase in bleeding time after aspirin is roughly two and a half minutes.

Researchers used to think that aspirin's effect on platelets would last up to one week after a single dose.[23,24] This led some to speculate that one might obtain an anticlotting result by giving aspirin every five to seven days. One small study suggests that might not be the case. Bleeding time actually begins to return to normal after 24 hours and reaches baseline by 48 hours.[25]

At this time no one can state with authority what the best aspirin program will be. Based on preliminary bleeding-time data, however, one could argue that one baby aspirin daily would be at least as good as (if not better than) one standard tablet every other day. It is even conceivable that a baby aspirin (81 mg) every other day would also provide some benefit. Always consult your physician for guidelines in your particular case.

Q. My husband currently takes one quarter of an aspirin every day. I'm concerned that his daily dose is not sufficient. He had heart surgery in 1984. Am I right to be worried?

A. Your husband may have hit on the optimal aspirin dose. Researchers are still trying to determine whether a baby aspirin (81 mg—roughly one fourth of the standard aspirin dose) is even more effective than one or more pills daily. Preliminary data suggests that less may be best.[26] Your husband should check with his cardiologist periodically to discuss his aspirin dose and have his bleeding time checked.

Q. In your *People's Pharmacy* newspaper column, you wrote that doctors found out aspirin was a real great thing back in the fifties. I have news for you. I knew about aspirin back in 1939. A doctor friend once told me aspirin-

was a blood thinner and people who use it are safe from heart attacks. I have used aspirin since 1940 (one tablet a day for 50 years).

Another thing. When you use aspirin you never get the flu—only small flu attacks but with aspirin in your system the virus is kept in check. I am 83 years old and still never had a real bad cold.

There is one other point I want to say: Users of aspirin have very good eyesight. No cataracts, etc. At my age I still read without glasses. Also users are protected against tumors of bowel or throat. The doctors have now found out that this is a real good drug, but I've known that for half a century. [February 7, 1992]

A. Thanks, Emil W. Elliott, from Maryland, for your fascinating observations. We still don't have the scientific data to confirm your points about cataracts, flu, colds, and throat cancer. But the rest of your story is right on target. And preliminary data does suggest that aspirin may stimulate the immune system and protect against cataracts. We don't know who your doctor friend was who recommended aspirin in 1939, but the first physician to write about such benefits was Dr. Lawrence L. Craven.

It all began with a chance observation of the Glendale, California, general practitioner. Shortly after the introduction of **Aspergum** in 1948, Dr. Craven started handing out packages of this aspirin-containing gum to his patients who had undergone tonsillectomy. He instructed them to chew one stick (containing 226.5 mg, or 3.5 grains aspirin) "one-half hour before each meal and at bedtime in order to enable them to eat and sleep well."[27]

Dr. Craven's regimen (just under three regular-strength tablets per day) did appear to provide some pain relief, but an unexpected problem occurred: " . . . several of my patients had serious postoperative hemorrhages which were difficult to control. The bleeding was sometimes so severe that hospitalization was necessary. In each instance the laboratory reported a prolonged coagulation time."[28]

After checking with these patients, Dr. Craven found that they had been so pleased with the **Aspergum**, they had purchased additional packets and were consuming extra sticks daily. It could have ended there, but Dr. Craven reviewed the medical literature of the time and discovered that salicylates had a powerful anticoagulant effect. He went on to speculate that ''if further study confirms the impression that acetylsalicylic acid prolongs coagulation time, it would appear that the drug might be of value as a preventive of vascular thrombotic conditions, including coronary thrombosis.''[29]

Dr. Craven soon put his theory into practice. In 1950 he reported that ''during the past two years, I have advised all of my male patients between the ages of 40 and 65 to take 10 to 30 grains [two to six regular-strength tablets] of aspirin daily as a possible preventive of coronary thrombosis. More than 400 have done so, and of these, none has suffered a coronary thrombosis.''[30]

Over the next six years Dr. Craven continued his research with smaller aspirin doses, encouraging friends and patients to take one tablet daily. He reported that this regimen could prevent heart attacks in otherwise healthy men or could prevent recurrences in those who had already suffered a coronary thrombosis.[31] By 1956 Dr. Craven reported that ''approximately 8,000 men have adopted a regime calling for from 5 to 10 gr. [one to two tablets] of aspirin daily, with a surprising result. Not a single case of detectable coronary or cerebral thrombosis has occurred among patients who faithfully have adhered to this regime.''[32]

Dr. Lawrence Craven's conclusions were almost completely ignored by the medical establishment. Harvard researchers did report in 1953 that arthritis patients who relied on aspirin to relieve their joint pain experienced a surprisingly low rate of heart attacks (less than 5 percent compared to 31 percent in the general population).[33] But most physicians were starting to focus their attention on cholesterol as the prime culprit in heart attacks. Cardiologists were admonishing patients to avoid eggs, milk, and cheese. Clot prevention (the ultimate cause of most heart attacks) was mostly ignored or forgotten.

It wasn't until the 1970s that large-scale aspirin studies began reappearing. Finally, in 1989 the American College of Chest Physicians recommended one aspirin daily for people at risk of coronary artery disease.

Dr. James E. Dalen, editor of the *Archives of Internal Medicine*, finally acknowledged Dr. Lawrence Craven's brilliance: "Looking back at Craven's reports, 40 years later and after dozens of clinical trials, what can we conclude? I would conclude that if his rule of an 'aspirin a day' had been adopted by Americans in 1950, hundreds of thousands of myocardial infarctions [heart attacks] and strokes might have been prevented."[34]

❑   ❑   ❑   ❑

References

1. Kannel, William B., and Wolf, Philip A. "Inferences from Secular Trend Analysis of Hypertension Control." *Am. J. Pub. Health* 1992; 82:1593–1595.

2. Ridker, Paul M. "Low-Dose Aspirin Therapy for Chronic Stable Angina: A Randomized, Placebo-Controlled Clinical Trial." *Ann. Int. Med.* 1991; 114:835–839.

3. Sherman, David G., et al. "Antithrombotic Therapy for Cerebrovascular Disorders. (Third ACCP Consensus Conference on Antithrombotic Therapy)." *Chest* 1992; 102:529S–538S.

4. Kannel, William B., op. cit.

5. *Morbidity and Mortality Chartbook on Cardiovascular, Lung and Blood Diseases—1990.* Bethesda, Md: National Heart, Lung and Blood Institute, 1990.

6. Casper, Michele, et al. "Antihypertensive Treatment and US Trends in Stroke Mortality, 1962 to 1980." *Am. J. Public Health* 1992; 82:1600–1606.

7. Leren, Paul, and Helgeland, Anders. "Coronary Heart Disease and Treatment of Hypertension." *Am. J. Med.* 1986; 80 (suppl. 2A):3–6.

8. Kannel, William B., op. cit.

9. The Dutch TIA Trial Study Group. "A Comparison of Two Doses of Aspirin (30 mg vs. 283 mg a Day) in Patients After a Transient Ischemic Attack or Minor Stroke." *N. Engl. J. Med.* 1991; 325:1261–1266.

10. Salonen, Jukka T., et al. "Clinical Investigation: High Stored Iron Levels Are Associated with Excess Risk of Myocardial Infarction in Eastern Finnish Men." *Circulation* 1992; 86:803–811.

11. Stipp, David. "Heart-Attack Study Adds to the Cautions About Iron in the Diet." *Wall Street Journal*, Sept. 8, 1992, p. 1.

12. Salonen, Jukka, T., op. cit.

13. Stipp, David, op. cit.

14. The Canadian Cooperative Study Group. "A Randomized Trial of Aspirin and Sulfinpyrazone in Threatened Stroke." *N. Engl. J. Med.* 1978; 299:53–59.

15. Bousser, M.G., et al. "AICLA Controlled Trial of Aspirin and Dipyridamole in the Secondary Prevention of Athero-Thrombotic Cerebral Ischemia." *Stroke* 1983; 14:5–14.

16. Manson, JoAnn E., et al. "A Prospective Study of Aspirin Use and Primary Prevention of Cardiovascular Disease in Women." *JAMA* 1991; 266:521–527.

17. Antiplatelet Trialists' Collaboration. "Secondary Prevention of Vascular Disease by Prolonged Antiplatelet Treatment." *Brit. Med. J.* 1988; 296:320–331.

18. UK-TIA Study Group. "United Kingdom Transient Attack (UK-TIA) Aspirin Trial: Interim Results." *Brit. Med. J.* 1988; 296:316–320.

19. The Dutch TIA Trial Study Group. "A Comparison of Two Doses of Aspirin (30 mg vs. 283 mg a Day) in Patients After a Transient Attack or Minor Ischemic Stroke." *N. Engl. J. Med.* 1991; 325:1261–1266.

20. Barnett, H.J.M. "Drug Treatment of Stroke and Ischemic Brain: From Acetylsalicylic Acid to New Drugs—100

Years of Pharmacology at Bayer Wuppertal-Eilberfeld: Aspirin in Stroke Prevention: An Overview." *Stroke* 1990; 21(12S):IV40–IV43.

21. Ibid.

22. Ibid.

23. Evans, G., Packham, M.A., et al. "The Effect of Acetylsalicylic Acid on Platelet Function." *J. Exp. Med.* 1968; 128: 877–894.

24. Weiss, H.J., et al. "The Effect of Salicylates on the Hemostatic Properties of Platelets in Man." *J. Clin. Invest.* 1968; 47:2169–2180.

25. Fiore, Louis D., et al. "The Bleeding Time Response to Aspirin." *Am. J. Clin. Pathol.* 1990; 94:292–296.

26. Ibid.

27. Craven, Lawrence L. "Acetylsalicylic Acid, Possible Preventive of Coronary Thrombosis." *Annals of Western Medicine* 1950; 4:95–99.

28. Ibid.

29. Ibid.

30. Ibid.

31. Craven, Lawrence L. "Experience with Aspirin (Acetylsalicylic Acid) in the Nonspecific Prophylaxis of Coronary Thrombosis." *Mississippi Valley Medical Journal* 1953; 75: 38–44.

32. Craven, Lawrence L. "Prevention of Coronary and Cerebral Thrombosis." *Mississippi Valley Medical Journal* 1956; 78: 213–215.

33. Cobb, Sidney, et al. "Length of Life and Causes of Death in Rheumatoid Arthritis." *N. Engl. J. Med.* 1953; 249:533–536.

34. Dalen, James E. "An Apple a Day or an Aspirin a Day?" *Arch. Intern. Med.* 1981; 151:1066–1069.

CHAPTER 9

USING ASPIRIN TO HELP PREVENT COLON CANCER

You can talk about heart attack and stroke prevention until you are blue in the face, but if you really want to catch someone's attention all you have to do is whisper that aspirin can prevent cancer. While the incidence of heart attack and stroke continue to plummet, cancer rates are climbing, especially for certain forms such as breast cancer and malignant melanoma. Colon cancer is one of the big killers. It is responsible for 12 percent of all cancer deaths in the United States.

Researchers have known for over a decade that aspirin and other nonsteroidal anti-inflammatory drugs (NSAIDs) could block the growth of cancer in rodents. These tumors were caused by administering artificial carcinogens.[1] The animals were also being given an NSAID. When the NSAID was stopped, the anticancer protection disappeared.[2] By 1988 there were epidemiological data that suggested aspirin could reduce colon and rectal cancer in humans, but because the work was carried out in Melbourne, Australia, it did not receive much attention in the United States.[3] Finally, in 1991, a report in the *Journal of the National Cancer Institute* concluded that regular use of aspirin could reduce colorectal cancer by 50 percent.[4]

But it apparently takes the seal of approval from the *New England Journal of Medicine* to really focus the attention of the medical profession and the media. That happened December 5, 1991, when Dr. Michael Thun and his colleagues at the American Cancer Society also reported a 40 to 50 percent reduction in fatal colon cancer in aspirin users.[5]

In 1992 epidemiologists for the American Cancer Society reported that men and women who ate fruits, vegetables, and high-fiber foods and also took at least 16 aspirin tablets a month had a greatly reduced risk of colon cancer (2.5 to 2.9 times less cancer).[6] An additional study confirmed that as little as one regular aspirin tablet a week could reduce colon cancer by 50 percent while daily aspirin "cut the risk by 63 percent."[7] Now that's impressive!

❑   ❑   ❑   ❑

Q. How can I use aspirin to prevent colon cancer?

A. First, let us hasten to warn you that while aspirin may help cut your risk of colon cancer, it is not an absolute guarantee. The accumulated data look fabulous so far, but we encourage you to talk to your doctor about the latest findings before you undertake a lifelong aspirin regimen.

Having issued that caution, however, we are happy to report that in one large epidemiological survey people "who used aspirin 16 or more times per month for at least one year" appeared to reduce their risk of colon cancer by roughly half.[8]

It is too early to be able to tell you the optimal dose or regimen to follow. At the time of this writing all we can say is that regular use (at least 4 times a week or 16 times a month) seems surprisingly effective. The most recent American Cancer Society findings suggest that eating lots of vegetables (carrots, tomatoes, potatoes, squash, corn, green leafies, cabbage, broccoli, brussels sprouts, etc.) and fruits along with taking aspirin can produce an even more impressive effect than aspirin alone.

Q. Colon cancer runs in my family, so I would appreciate a complete explanation of what we know about how aspirin can help prevent it and all the physiology involved.

A. The story of aspirin against cancer got its start back in the early 1980s. Rats and other animals treated with carcinogens often develop tumors of the colon. This is thought to be a good model for human colon cancer since the tumors are biologically similar. When the animals were also treated with NSAIDs (nonsteroidal anti-inflammatory drugs) like aspirin, **Indocin** (indomethacin), **Feldene** (piroxicam), and **Clinoril** (sulindac), there was "inhibition of the growth of colon tumors."[9,10,11,12]

This fascinating discovery led to several small clinical studies in humans. Investigators found that people who are genetically predisposed to develop polyps (and are therefore at greater risk of colorectal cancer) could make the precancerous growths "regress" when they took Clinoril.[13]

The stage was set for epidemiological studies. Researchers analyzed drug use from several large data bases. The investigators found that regular use of NSAIDs (including aspirin) appeared to roughly halve the incidence of colorectal cancer.[14,15,16] It may also improve survival if cancer occurs.

How are aspirin and other NSAIDs working this magic? It's far too early to know for sure, but current studies suggest that the connection may involve those hormonelike chemicals, the prostaglandins. Prostaglandins are responsible for uterine contractions during labor and play a critical role in the process of inflammation and pain associated with sprains, strains, and arthritis. Blocking the prostaglandin-making machinery with aspirin is thought to be the prime mechanism for pain relief. But prostaglandins may also be key players in some cancers. One current hypothesis is that by knocking out prostaglandins, aspirin (and other NSAIDs) may suppress cell growth necessary for tumor formation.[17,18] These drugs may also indirectly stimulate the immune system.[19]

Q. We have a history of colon cancer in our family and I'm taking low-dose aspirin as a preventive. Should I also be giving aspirin to my children, ages 9 and 14?

A. We would discourage you from giving aspirin to your children despite your family history. They will be at relatively low risk for many years to come. Hopefully, we will have a better understanding of the whole process before they pass into the higher-risk age group. And there is always the risk of Reye's syndrome when giving aspirin regularly to children.

Q. In the Boston Study of colorectal cancer, how much aspirin was taken and for how long? Were the subjects men and women or just men?

A. The "Boston" study actually involved patients from hospitals in Boston, New York, Philadelphia, and Baltimore. Both men and women were included in the investigation. Since it was not a "prospective" study in that aspirin was not administered in a double-blind controlled manner, we cannot establish any single dose. This "case-control" type of research merely analyzes the drug-taking behavior of these people (through use of questionnaires) and matches it with the incidence of cancer.

The researchers found that "regular use" of aspirin or other NSAIDs (defined as four times a week for at least three months in the year prior to the study) reduced the risk of colorectal cancer by about 50 percent. People who had been taking it but then stopped aspirin in the year before the study experienced no such benefit.

Q. I have colon cancer on both sides of my family, so I am eager to learn how I can cut my risk by taking aspirin. What is the best type of aspirin to take and how much?

A. No one yet has a definitive answer to this question. It may be that roughly one tablet every other day will be adequate. Perhaps even one tablet a week will work. The largest study to date involved 764,343 men and women. The researchers found that when aspirin was used at least 16 times per month for at least one year, colon cancer was 2.4 to 2.9 times less common.

Q. I had surgery for colon cancer in 1987. Should I be taking aspirin to prevent a recurrence?

A. This is a question that only your physician can answer for sure. To be certain he or she is up on the latest aspirin research, you may wish to take along a copy of the original work published in the *Journal of the National Cancer Institute* and the *New England Journal of Medicine*.[20,21] Then have a frank discussion about the pros and cons of aspirin as a preventive for colon cancer. It may be that the benefits are worth the risks since there is some indication from animal research that the drug may both prevent and reverse tumor growth. But only your doctor will know what is best in your specific situation.

Q. Has aspirin been found useful in preventing or treating any kinds of cancer other than colon cancer?

A. New research from The American Cancer Society suggests that aspirin is also effective in reducing the risk of cancer of the stomach and esophagus. We wouldn't be surprised to learn in the next couple of years that aspirin helps reduce the risk of other cancers as well.

❑   ❑   ❑   ❑

References

1. Baron, John A., and Greenberg, E. Robert. "Could Aspirin Really Prevent Colon Cancer?" *N. Engl. J. Med.* 1991; 325:1644–1645.
2. Reddy, B.S., et al. "Dose-Related Inhibition of Colon Carcinogenesis by Dietary Piroxicam, a Nonsteroidal Anti-

inflammatory Drug, During Different States of Rat Colon Tumor Development." *Cancer Res.* 1987; 47:5340–5346.

3. Kune, G.A., et al. "Colorectal Cancer Risk, Chronic Illnesses, Operations, and Medications: Case Control Results from the Melbourne Colorectal Cancer Study." *Cancer Res.* 1988; 48:4399–4404.

4. Rosenberg, L., et al. "A Hypothesis: Nonsteroidal Anti-Inflammatory Drugs Reduce the Incidence of Large-Bowel Cancer. *J. Natl. Cancer Inst.* 1991; 83:355–358.

5. Thun, Michael J., et al. "Aspirin Use and Reduced Risk of Fatal Colon Cancer." *N. Engl. J. Med.* 1991; 325:1593–1594.

6. Thun, Michael J., et al. *J. Natl. Cancer Inst.* 1992; 84:1491–1500.

7. Late News. "Aspirin May Cut Colon Cancer Risk by 50 Percent." *Modern Medicine* 1992; 33(11):9.

8. Thun, Michael J., 1991, op. cit.

9. Pollard, M., and Luckert, P.H. "Indomethacin Treatment of Rats with Dimethylhydrazine-Induced Intestinal Tumors." *Cancer Treat. Rep.* 1980; 64:1323–1327.

10. Reddy, B.S., et al., op. cit.

11. Metzger, U., et al. Influence of Various Prostaglandin Synthesis Inhibitors on DMH-Induced Rat Colon Cancer." *Dis. Colon Rectum* 1984; 27:366–369.

12. Moorghen, M., et al. "The Effect of Sulindac on Colonic Tumor Formation in Dimethylhydrazine-Treated Mice." *Acta Histochem. Suppl.* 1990; 39:195–199.

13. Labayle, D., et al. "Sulindac Causes Regression of Rectal Polyps in Familial Adenomatous Polyposis." *Gastroenterology* 1991; 101:635–639.

14. Rosenberg, Lynn, et al. "A Hypothesis: Nonsteroidal Anti-Inflammatory Drugs Reduce the Incidence of Large-Bowel Cancer." *J. Natl. Cancer Inst.* 1991; 83:355–358.

15. Thun, Michael J., op. cit.

16. Kune, G.A., et al. "Colorectal Cancer Risk, Chronic Illnesses, Operations, and Medications: Case Control Results from the Melbourne Colorectal Cancer Study." *Cancer* 1988; 48:4399–4404.

17. Lupulescu, A. "Enhancement of Carcinogenesis by Prostaglandins." *Nature* 1978; 270:634–636.

18. Lynch, N.R., et al. "Mechanism of Inhibition of Tumour Growth by Aspirin and Indomethacin." *Br. J. Cancer* 1978; 38:503–512.

19. Plescia, O.J., et al. "Subversion of Immune System by Tumor Cells and the Role of Prostaglandins." *Proc. Natl. Acad. Sci.* 1975; 75:1848–1851.

20. Thun, Michael J., 1992, op. cit.

21. Thun, Michael J., 1991, op. cit.

CHAPTER 10

OTHER USES FOR ASPIRIN

This chapter is a roundup of other possible, actual, or imagined uses for aspirin. It represents an eclectic mixture of aspirin lore, with and without scientific validation.

❑   ❑   ❑   ❑

Q. Can an aspirin tablet dissolved in water help cut flowers last longer? My grandmother swears by this trick but I can't tell the difference. What about aspirin for Christmas trees? Anything that would help them last longer would be welcome.

A. The great gurus at *The Wall Street Journal* suggest that if you put one aspirin in a vase, "your flowers will last longer. (They reduce the rate at which the leaves lose moisture to the air.) Put some in your Christmas tree stand, and the tree will last longer."[1]

We could find no scientific data to support these popular beliefs. Teresa and Joe's daughter (Alena Graedon) actually did a science project for fifth grade comparing the effects of birth control pills, **BC Powder** (containing aspirin and salicylamide), fertilizer, and plain water on the growth of radish seeds. To her surprise, the radishes treated with birth control pills grew taller and faster. Those treated with **BC** did the least well. This may not be a fair test of aspirin for cut flowers, but it suggests you shouldn't water your live plants with aspirin.

Q. Can taking a couple of aspirin with a glass of warm milk help you get to sleep?

A. We have never found any data to support the common belief that aspirin relieves insomnia. Lots of folks tell us that aspirin helps them to fall asleep, but it makes no sense pharmacologically. Aspirin has no known sedative effects. Then again, if you had asked us ten years ago if aspirin could reduce the risk of cataracts, colon cancer, or eclampsia, we would have laughed. We have learned never to discount the power of aspirin.

We suspect, though, that it is the milk rather than the aspirin that is providing benefit. Milk contains tryptophan, a building block of the brain chemical serotonin, which is important for sleep. People who suffer from arthritis or other chronic pain conditions may benefit from nighttime aspirin if the pain is keeping them awake.

Q. Can aspirin be used to help treat high blood pressure?

A. There is no evidence that aspirin will help control garden variety hypertension. Although there is no data to cause concern, it is theoretically possible that high doses of aspirin might even produce a mild increase in blood pressure.[2]

There is good news for one very special kind of blood pressure problem, though. A significant number of women develop hypertension during pregnancy. This can be a very serious situation for both mother and baby. Low doses of aspirin have been found surprisingly effective at controlling pregnancy-induced hypertension. Of course, no pregnant woman should take any drug, including aspirin, without her physician's approval and careful supervision.

Q. If you gargle with aspirin, will it relieve a sore throat? My dad has been doing this for years and he insists that it is the best sore throat remedy there is.

A. Here is a folk belief that may actually have some scientific grounding. When one of us was a graduate student in pharmacology (Joe Graedon), the professor who taught about salicylates insisted that aspirin was ineffective for tooth pain or sore throats. He maintained that **Aspergum** did not provide any local benefit in the mouth or throat and could only exert its action "systemically." What he meant was that when you chewed the **Aspergum** the aspirin would be released, swallowed, and end up in the stomach, where it would eventually be absorbed into the bloodstream and then produce pain relief.

Well, we have discovered that when aspirin is used in a gargle after tonsillectomy, it does appear to provide some relief.[3] More recently, British oral surgeons and pharmacologists studied the effect of placing aspirin into the tooth socket after impacted third molars were extracted. To our surprise, they found that local application of aspirin was "an effective method for control of pain in the early postoperative period, without interference with the normal healing process."[4] We still warn people against applying an aspirin tablet directly to a toothache. Dentists tell us that it can damage gum tissue and be very irritating within the mouth.

Q. My wife insists on taking aspirin every time she has a cold or the flu. I keep telling her this is useless, but she won't believe me. What do you think?

A. We side with you. Popular wisdom to the contrary, aspirin is not all that great for relieving cold symptoms. High fever and muscle aches are relatively uncommon consequences of the common cold, and therefore aspirin probably won't make anyone feel substantially better.

There is even some preliminary evidence that taking aspirin for a cold could be counterproductive. Investigators at the University of Illinois College of Medicine found that aspirin increased "virus shedding" in nasal secretions by as much as 38 percent. These scientists concluded, "Aspirin treatment, which permits the person to stay on the job with more infectious secretions, should make him a greater epidemiological hazard."[5]

On the other hand, aspirin may be helpful against influenza. There are some preliminary data that suggest aspirin boosts the antibody reponse to a flu shot. Aspirin may also increase the body's natural flu fighters—interleukins and interferons. More research is necessary to reveal how helpful or harmful aspirin really is against viral infections.

Q. I have heard that scientists have discovered that aspirin can help prevent cataracts. Is there anything to this?

A. We only wish we could provide a clear "yes or no" answer to this important question. A number of small studies carried out both in animals and in people suggest that aspirin may indeed be able to delay the onset or reduce the risk of cataracts.[6,7,8,9]

A Romanian researcher, for example, has noted that patients with rheumatoid arthritis treated with aspirin for long periods of time appeared far less likely to develop cataracts.[10] The same kind of observation was made back in the 1950s with regard to rheumatoid arthritis and heart attacks.[11]

It has been known for decades that diabetics and people who take cortisone-type medications have a high incidence of cataracts. It is proposed that sugar and corticosteroids bind to "crystallins" (proteinlike groups of amino acids) in the lens of the eye to cause cloudiness. Ophthalmologist Edward Cotlier has found that aspirin prevents the binding of glucose and certain steroids to lysine crystallins. An antioxidant effect of aspirin may also be working to block cataract formation.[12]

Having said all this, however, it must be noted that a well-designed recent study sponsored by the National Eye Institute did not demonstrate any beneficial effect of aspirin on cataract development in diabetics.[13] Only time and more research will reveal if aspirin truly does have a positive effect on the eyes.

Q. Do people who take aspirin regularly have fewer gallstones? Can aspirin be used to prevent them?

A. The data do not exist to answer these questions adequately. One study of 4,524 patients taking 1,000 mg of aspirin a day showed no reduced hospitalization for gallstones.[14] In other words, aspirin did not seem to prevent gallbladder problems. And yet experimental data and several small studies suggest that aspirin might help prevent the development of gallstones.[15] It could be several years before this apparent contradiction is resolved.

Q. Will aspirin prevent senility? My grandmother is in a nursing home. She can't recognize anyone in the family. Sometimes I don't think she even knows who she is. If aspirin could prevent that from happening, I would start taking it tomorrow.

A. Aspirin may play a valuable role in the prevention of senile dementia. A pilot study has shown that low doses of aspirin can improve thought processes in people with multi-infarct dementia. This kind of senility is brought on by the formation of tiny multiple blood clots in the brain. By preventing these clots, the researchers were able to demonstrate improved blood flow to the brain as well as better scores on cognitive tests, especially for women.[16]

There is even the possibility that aspirin may play a positive role against Alzheimer's disease. Dr. Patrick McGeer is a professor of psychiatry at the University of British Columbia in Vancouver. He has proposed that "an aspirin a day might keep the gerontologists away."[17] During a brainstorming session at the National Institute of Aging, Dr. McGeer suggested that aspirin might help prevent inflammatory reactions that could be causing cell membrane disruption and leading to the death of neurons. He noted that

"I've never seen a rheumatoid arthritis patient with signs of Alzheimer's on autopsy."[18]

It is still far too early to know if small doses of aspirin will actually provide any benefit either in helping to prevent this dread disease or contributing to improvement once it is diagnosed. If the preliminary hypothesis holds up, however, it could be the greatest contribution aspirin has made yet.

Q. What effective use, if any, could aspirin have on Crohn's disease?

A. Probably none. There is no indication that aspirin provides any relief for symptoms of inflammatory bowel disease. A derivative (a chemical cousin), however, called 5-aminosalicylic acid (5-ASA) is used for this often painful condition. The most commonly prescribed medicine, sulfasalazine (**Azulfidine**) delivers 5-ASA to the bowel, where it provides some symptomatic control for this disease.

Q. When I overdo it on exercise and it feels like all my muscles are aching simultaneously, I throw half a dozen aspirin tablets into the bath tub, turn on the hot water, and then take a long hot soak. Is there any danger that I might absorb the aspirin into my body and experience a toxic reaction?

A. Boy, that is one aspirin use we had never heard of before. It doesn't seem likely that enough aspirin could be absorbed into your body to do harm, though we fear the aspirin might be irritating to your skin. We're actually a little surprised that you claim success for this treatment, but as we have said before, when it comes to aspirin, almost nothing surprises us anymore. Could it be that the hot water soak is what is really relieving those sore muscles?

Q. After one normal pregnancy, I experienced two miscarriages in the first trimester. My doctor did a blood

test for something he called lupus factor. The test was inconclusive, but he recommended that I take one baby aspirin per day to prevent possible future miscarriages. Can you explain what this is all about?

A. Pregnant women are usually advised to avoid aspirin, especially in the last trimester. The fear is that aspirin could increase the risk of fetal hemorrhage or a life-threatening bleeding episode for the mother during labor and delivery. In the last few years, though, many obstetricians have been prescribing low-dose (60 mg to 150 mg daily) aspirin to actually prevent certain problems of pregnancy.

Miscarriages can be caused by many different factors. One of those can be high blood pressure, known as PIH (pregnancy-induced hypertension), formerly referred to as preeclampsia. It can lead to poor fetal growth, in part because of reduced circulation to the placenta. Another complication can be autoimmune diseases like lupus, which put women at higher risk because of a tendency for blood to clot.

When prescribed by a physician, small doses of aspirin appear to reduce the risk of pregnancy-induced hypertension. Another positive outcome is improvement in birth weight. Aspirin may also diminish the risk of blood clots. This may be why your OB/GYN suggested aspirin since your blood test wasn't completely normal.

Q. Can aspirin be used to treat painful attacks of gout? If so, does it help relieve the underlying disease or just mask the symptoms?

A. Gout is caused by a buildup of uric acid within the body. When levels of this compound get too high, urate crystals can precipitate in and around joints, leading to swelling, redness, and excruciating pain. The big toe is a common location for gout attacks, but knees, insteps, ankles, wrists, and elbows are also targets.

Aspirin can have important effects on uric acid levels, depending upon the amount you swallow. Standard doses of three to six regular-strength tablets a day (1 to 2 grams of aspirin) may actually make gout worse by raising uric acid levels in the blood. Large doses (more than 5 grams or 15 pills) can actually speed the elimination of uric acid from the body and lower urate in the bloodstream. This means that the underlying disease process is actually being controlled. The only problem is that at such high doses there are serious risks of stomach irritation and ulceration. Never take large aspirin doses without medical supervision!

Aspirin can also block the benefits of other gout treatments, so it should never be taken by someone who is also relying on medicine like probenecid (**Benemid, Col-BENEMID, Probalan, Robenedic**, etc.) or sulfinpyrazone (**Anturane**).

Q. Two years ago, I had an attack of phlebitis in the superficial veins of my leg. You could see the two clots, each one the size of a robin's egg. My doctor recommended ibuprofen and bed rest, but after four days there was no improvement, so I consulted a vascular specialist at New York-Cornell Medical Center. He told me to take six aspirins per day for two weeks, then four aspirins per day, then two per day as needed. In just a few days both clots went away and I was back to work.

A. Wow! Pretty darn impressive. Aspirin does possess anti-imflammatory action, and of course it has strong anti-clotting potential. This is not a project others should try on their own, however.

Q. I have an enlarged prostate. Can aspirin eliminate or delay the need for prostate surgery?

A. There is no evidence that aspirin can shrink the prostate or diminish the need for surgery. There are several other prescription medications that may be of benefit here. They include **Hytrin** (terazosin), **Minipress** (prazosin), and **Cardura** (doxazosin). **Proscar** (finasteride), a new drug that is supposed to help shrink the prostate, may also be of some benefit. You need to discuss your situation with a good urologist.

Q. For the past year I have been waking up with night sweats. The other night I took two aspirin for back pain and noticed that my night sweats were much diminished. Can aspirin affect this condition and, if so, why and how?

A. Night sweats can be caused by a number of different conditions. It is important to find out what is behind this uncomfortable symptom. We can't explain why aspirin might be helpful in relieving your discomfort.

Q. My daughter has multiple sclerosis. Can she benefit from aspirin or should she avoid it?

A. This is a more complicated question than you might think. Patients with MS appear to have a number of cellular changes—from immune system and neurological abnormalities to blood cell differences. Aspirin may modify some of the biochemical changes seen in blood. Whether this is helpful remains to be established. We could not find any reference to special danger from aspirin. Nevertheless, your daughter should not take aspirin except under medical supervision.

Q. Can aspirin be used to treat or prevent varicose veins?

A. Doctors don't know what causes varicose veins or how to prevent them. One possible complication of this disorder is thrombophlebitis (blood clots in veins). Although it is unlikely that aspirin can prevent varicose veins (there have been no studies designed specifically to answer this question), it might help keep blood clots from forming. Please ask your physician if she thinks aspirin would be helpful.

A reanalysis of the Physicians' Health Study data produced a fascinating observation. Circulatory problems in arms and legs were markedly reduced in aspirin takers. Surgery was far less common in these people.[19] It is conceivable that clotting and other complications associated with varicose veins might be diminished by alternate-day aspirin use. Naturally such a question is best directed toward a vascular specialist until solid clinical data becomes available.

Q. I have heard that aspirin can help eliminate certain problems of pregnancy. But I would hate to take *any* drug at all now that I am pregnant. What do you advise?

A. You should never take any drug during pregnancy unless it has been specifically approved by your obstetrician. Doctors sometimes prescribe aspirin for women whose blood pressure begins to rise during pregnancy. Small aspirin doses (60 to 150 mg) per day appear to be very effective in preventing pregnancy-induced hypertension (PIH) and severe low birth weight in newborns. Researchers speculate that it is the process of knocking out thromboxane A_2 while preserving prostacyclin that has produced this beneficial outcome.[20] If you have a normal, healthy pregnancy, though, aspirin need not be an issue for you.

Q. My wife takes high-dose aspirin for a painful chronic back problem. What doses and/or forms of aspirin (or other similar drugs) would give her maximum relief?

A. The recommended dose for back problems is the same as that for any inflammatory disorder—two to three regular-strength tablets every four hours. The maximum amount considered safe by the the Food and Drug Administration is 4,000 mg (12 regular-strength tablets) in one day. Keep in mind that at this dose, she may be at some risk of stomach irritation or ulceration.

Q. My husband routinely uses aspirin and a cold pack to relieve the pain of his bad back. Is it a good idea to combine the cold pack with aspirin?

A. Either cold or heat can be a useful addition to aspirin in the treatment of muscle sprain or strain. For years, health professionals have been arguing about whether cold packs or heat packs work best. Current consensus seems to be that cold is often particularly useful within 24 hours of an acute injury. After that period, each individual should experiment to determine whether heat or cold—or some combination of the two—works best.

❑   ❑   ❑   ❑

References

1. Dolan, Carrie. "What Soothes Aches, Makes Flowers Last, And Grows Hair?" *Wall Street Journal,* Feb. 19, 1988, p. 1.

2. Frolich, J.C. "Prostacyclin in Hypertension." *Z. Kardiol.* 1992; 81:303–309.

3. Ballantyne, J. "Tonsillectomy by Dissection," in Ballantyne, J., ed. *Operative Surgery: Nose and Throat,* 3rd ed. London: Butterworths, 1976, pp. 153–157.

4. Moore, Undrell J., et al. "The Efficacy of Locally Applied Aspirin and Acetaminophen in Postoperative Pain After Third Molar Surgery." *Clin. Pharmacol. Ther.* 1992; 52: 292–296.

5. Stanley, Edith D., et al. "Increased Virus Shedding with Aspirin Treatment of Rhinovirus Infection." *JAMA* 1975; 231:1248–1251.

6. Blakytny, R., and Harding, J.J. "Prevention of Cataract in Diabetic Rats by Aspirin, Paracetamol (Acetaminophen) and Ibuprofen." *Exp. Eye Research* 1992; 54:509–518.

7. Sharma, Y.R., et al. "Systemic Aspirin and Systemic Vitamin E in Senile Cataracts: Cataract V." *Indian J. Ophthalmol.* 1989; 37:134–141.

8. Harding, J.J., et al. "Protection Against Cataract by Aspirin, Paracetamol and Ibuprofen." *Acta Ophthalmol.* 1989; 67: 518–524.

9. Harding, J.J., and van Heyningen, R. "Epidemiology and Risk Factors for Cataract." *Eye* 1987; 1:537–541.

10. Mihail, S. "Aspirin in the Preventive Treatment of Cataract." *Oftalmologia* 1990; 34:43–46.

11. Cobb, Sidney, et al. "Length of Life and Causes of Death in Theumatoid Arthritis." *N. Engl. J. Med.* 1953; 249:533–536.

12. Cotlier, Edward. "Acetylation of Lens Crystallins and Prevention of Diabetic and Steroid Cataracts." *Aspirin Towards 2000,* from the European Aspirin Foundation.

13. Chew, E.Y., et al. "Aspirin Effects on the Development of Cataracts in Patients with Diabetes Mellitus. Early Treatment Diabetic Retinopathy Study Report 16." *Arch. Ophthalmol.* 1992; 110:339–342.

14. Kurata, J.H., et al. "One Gram of Aspirin Per Day Does Not Reduce Risk of Hospitalization for Gallstone Disease." *Dig. Dis. Sci.* 1991; 36:1110–1115.

15. Heller, F.R. "Sludge, Gallstones and Aspirin." *Acta Gastroenterol. Belg.* 1990; 53:16–21.

16. "Aspirin and Multi-Infarct Dementia." *Physicians' Drug Alerts.* 1989; Aug.:58.

17. Pollner, Fran. "Alzheimer's Disease." *Medical World News* 1990; 12 Feb.:16–17.

18. Ibid.

19. Goldhaber, Samuel Z., et al. "Low-Dose Aspirin and Subsequent Peripheral Arterial Surgery in the Physicians' Health Study." *Lancet* 1992; 340:143–145.

20. Imperiale, Thomas F., and Stollenwerk Petrulis, Alice. "A Meta-analysis of Low-Dose Aspirin for the Prevention of Pregnancy-Induced Hypertensive Disease." *JAMA* 1991; 266:261–265.

III

SIDE EFFECTS, GUIDELINES, & PRECAUTIONS

CHAPTER 11

ASPIRIN AND YOUR STOMACH

As great as aspirin is, our favorite wonder drug does have a major downside—tummy trouble. Users of natural forms of aspirin in the 1800s complained that it was like having fire ants in the belly.[1] Times haven't changed much. Aspirin still causes a high incidence of indigestion, heartburn, stomach pain, loss of appetite, and nausea, in roughly 5 to 25 percent of users. It can also bring on ulcers, which can be serious indeed. Anyone with a sensitive stomach will likely have to avoid aspirin. So should people with ulcers, especially bleeding ulcers.

Every dose of aspirin causes a little loss of blood from the stomach wall. It usually amounts to about half a teaspoonful—usually nothing to get excited about. But over time, this may lead to iron deficiency anemia. Older people can be especially vulnerable to this condition and need to have frequent blood tests to make sure they aren't getting into trouble.

Most people don't realize that regular aspirin use can lead to such serious stomach trouble that it could be fatal for some people. Approximately 20 percent of patients taking NSAIDs (nonsteroidal anti-inflammatory drugs) on a regular basis develop gastric ulcers. We are talking about drugs such as aspirin, **Anaprox, Ansaid, Clinoril, Dolobid, Feldene, Indocin, Lodine, Meclomen, Motrin, Nalfon, Naprosyn, Orudis, Relafen, Tolectin,** and **Voltaren**.

According to Dr. James Fries, associate professor of medicine, division of immunology and rheumatology at Stanford University School of Medicine, NSAIDs (including aspirin) account "for more than 70,000 hospitalizations and 7,000 deaths annually in the United States."[2] The Food and Drug Administration has estimated the risk may be even higher—10,000 to 20,000 deaths annually.[3] To put this into perspective, keep in mind that deaths from these arthritis drugs are far more common than for all illicit drugs combined. That includes heroin, crack, cocaine, marijuana, etc. Dr. Fries has gone so far as to call the NSAID-induced digestive disorders a toxic "epidemic."

Peptic ulcers, bleeding ulcers, and perforated ulcers can be life threatening. Worst of all, people with ulcers may not know they are in trouble. For some people, the first sign of an ulcer is massive bleeding. But others do have some advance warning. Feeling full before eating the usual amount, feeling tired and low in energy, losing weight when you're not doing anything differently, and suffering chronic indigestion or heartburn may be red flags to check in with the doctor. The moral of this tale is to treat aspirin and all NSAIDs with great respect. Have regular medical checkups. At the first sign of symptoms, call your physician for help!

Protecting your stomach isn't easy, but there are several tricks to try to lessen the damage. First, dissolve your aspirin before you take it. The little chunks that may lodge in your stomach can be especially irritating to sensitive tissues. Some doctors have recommended chewing your tablets before swallowing, and then washing the residue down with milk. We have never found this very appealing. Another alternative is to drop your aspirin tablets into a glass of fizzy water (carbonated mineral water) for about five or ten minutes. They bounce around a bit as they disintegrate. Be sure to drink *all* the water you dissolved them in, so you get the full dose. In fact, a full 8 ounces of water to wash down aspirin any time you take it is a wise precaution.

What about buffered or enteric-coated tablets? The enteric-coated tablets can certainly help, as they don't dissolve until they reach the lower part of the digestive tract. Don't take them with milk or food, though, as that might counteract the enteric coating by letting it dissolve in the stomach. Some people may find that buffered tablets are less likely to cause digestive upset, but those who must take large doses, or those who take aspirin every day, may not get enough stomach protection from the buffers added to these tablets.

There are some alternate medications that appear less likely to irritate the gut than aspirin is. The non-aspirin salicylates, such as salsalate (**Artha-G, Disalcid, Mono-Gesic**, etc.) or choline magnesium trisalicylate (**Trilisate**) can reduce inflammation. **Trilisate** and **Arthropan** (choline salicylate) are available in a liquid formulation that might prove less irritating. **Arthropan** can be purchased over the counter, but the others require a prescription, so check with your doctor.

Another alternative that the doctor might suggest for those on aspirin to treat arthritis pain is an occasional "drug holiday." Taking a brief break from daily aspirin consumption may give sensitive stomach tissue a chance to repair the damage. Your physician can advise you how long these drug holidays should be, and how often they should be taken. He or she will also have suggestions for managing the pain while you are not taking aspirin. Acetaminophen (**Anacin-3, APAP, Panadol, Tylenol**, etc.) may offer the necessary pain relief during this time.

The doctor may also want to prescribe an anti-ulcer medicine, such as **Carafate** (sucralfate), to be taken on a regular basis to try to prevent stomach damage and ulceration. This approach is somewhat controversial, as it's not clear that these drugs are highly effective in warding off aspirin irritation.

At least one prescription medication was developed expressly to guard against irritation due to aspirin and other

NSAIDs. Because much of the problem seems to stem from aspirin's ability to interfere with prostaglandins that protect the stomach lining, researchers looked for a medicine that could add that prostaglandin back. **Cytotec** (misoprostol) is that drug. Doctors are especially likely to prescribe it for arthritis patients having trouble with their pain medicines. It can work well, but it does have a number of side effects that may be hard to handle. Many people report that it causes severe diarrhea and stomachaches. It can also cause headaches, nausea, dizziness, and constipation. It must never be taken during pregnancy, as it could induce premature labor. Despite these drawbacks, **Cytotec** has been a boon for some aspirin users.

❑   ❑   ❑   ❑

Q. Aspirin irritates my stomach, but I would like to take it in small doses to prevent heart attacks and colorectal cancer. So I would like information on how, when, and what types to take to avoid stomach irritation.

A. Stomach irritation, gastritis, ulcers, and perforation of the stomach wall are all very serious complications of aspirin therapy. A perforated ulcer can be a life-threatening situation.

Does this mean that people with tender tummies can never benefit from the protective action of aspirin? Not necessarily. The bottom line is that you may need to experiment to find out what approach is right for you. But while you are doing this, you must keep a number of points in mind:

1. **Stomach irritation is usually dose-dependent. But some people can get into trouble even with tiny amounts.**
2. **Aspirin may irritate the stomach through both direct and indirect routes.**

3. Special forms of aspirin may help prevent direct irritation, but not indirect irritation.
4. Anyone who takes aspirin on a regular basis needs medical supervision. This is especially true for those with sensitive stomachs.

Q. What do you mean when you say that stomach upset is dose-dependent?

A. We simply mean that the more aspirin you swallow, the more likely you will develop digestive upset. Someone who takes six to ten tablets daily for arthritis symptoms will be more likely to experience heartburn than the person who takes only one baby aspirin (81 mg) a day. And the person who takes half a baby aspirin (40 mg) or one baby aspirin every other day should be less likely to get into trouble than the individual who takes it daily. Having said that, however, we hasten to add that some susceptible people can experience heartburn, indigestion, and ulcers on even half a baby aspirin.

Q. So what about those special forms of aspirin—buffered aspirin, coated aspirin, soluble aspirin (such as Alka-Seltzer) or other products designed to lessen stomach upset?

A. Millions swallow such formulations daily in the hope that they will be able to bypass GI irritation. And to some degree these products may help some people. They are not, however, a guarantee against trouble.

Q. What do you mean when you say aspirin can irritate the stomach by two routes: direct and indirect?

A. Aspirin causes stomach problems through two primary mechanisms. First, aspirin is directly irritating by surface contact. Anyone who puts an aspirin tablet directly on an aching tooth, for example, will risk irritating the tender gum tissue. It is possible to reduce this direct irritation by a variety of methods we will discuss below. The longer the particles of aspirin stay in contact with the stomach lining, the greater the likelihood of damage.

The second way aspirin causes stomach upset is indirect. You could inject aspirin straight into a vein or insert a suppository in your rectum and this drug could still be toxic to the stomach.

Q. OK. I can understand how aspirin can upset my stomach by direct contact. But please explain the indirect pathway by which it produces irritation.

A. To understand this indirect pathway to GI pain, you have to go back and review how aspirin works. The prevailing theory is that aspirinlike drugs (including ibuprofen and most prescription arthritis medicines) block the manufacture of natural substances called prostaglandins. Certain prostaglandins are involved in the inflammatory and pain reaction experienced after trauma such as a sprain or strain. They also contribute to the discomfort of arthritis. By blocking prostaglandin synthesis, aspirin can reduce pain and inflammation.

But prostaglandins also protect the stomach lining. They do this two ways: first by limiting acid production in the stomach, and more importantly, by stimulating the secretion of mucus. It is mucus that stops the stomach from digesting itself. Without that mucus layer the stomach becomes much more vulnerable to damage. After all, this is an incredibly hostile environment. Just think of the acid and other chemicals floating around in your gut that are necessary to digest food. If you were to take a few drops of that stomach acid and put them on this page, they would eat a hole right through it. It's no wonder then that arthritis medicines that suppress prostaglandins and diminish the mucus coating often create conditions that lead to ulcers.

Q. All right. Now explain the methods you can use to block the direct irritation caused by aspirin.

A. There are a number of strategies you can use to reduce the direct irritation of your stomach by aspirin:

1. **Using coated aspirin**
2. **Taking aspirin with food or water**
3. **Using buffered aspirin or antacids**
4. **Crushing your aspirin tablets before taking them**
5. **Taking aspirin in powdered (soluble) form**
6. **Dissolving aspirin in water or juice before taking it**
7. **Using aspirin suppositories**
8. **Using liquid effervescent aspirin**

Q. Could you run through those options one by one?

A. Let's start with coated aspirin (**Ecotrin, A.S.A. Enseals, Easprin**, enteric-coated generic aspirin, etc.). The coating is designed to allow the tablet to bypass the stomach intact and be dissolved in the small intestine where it is less likely to cause damage. Unfortunately, some coated aspirin is erratic in absorption. Some pills have been reported to dissolve too soon (in the stomach), while others may dissolve late and may not produce rapid blood levels of salicylate. One doctor we know jokes that enough coated aspirin pills have passed into the plumbing systems of America to make sure our pipes will never have arthritis.

Q. How about taking your aspirin with milk, water, juice, or food?

A. Taking aspirin with snacks or at mealtime is another effective way to diminish irritation. But swallowing aspirin on a full stomach may also delay absorption and slow pain relief.

Don't take aspirin with orange juice or any other acidic beverage. Aspirin dissolves best in an alkaline medium. Milk would be a good choice. But liquid volume is equally important. Try to swallow your aspirin with a full eight ounces of water to maximize absorption and decrease direct irritation.

Q. How about buffered aspirin?

A. Buffered aspirins usually contain one or more antacids along with acetylsalicylic acid. Products like **Arthritis Strength Bufferin, Alka-Seltzer, Ascriptin, Bufferin**, and **Cama Arthritis Pain Reliever** are all sold with the implied promise that they will somehow protect the stomach. And to a degree they may.

Antacids like aluminum and magnesium hydroxide, calcium carbonate, and sodium bicarbonate do help neutralize stomach acid by raising pH. This enhances dissolution of aspirin tablets and improves absorption. The theory is that if the tablets break down faster, there will be less contact between undissolved chunks of aspirin and sensitive stomach tissue. These particles are thought to be especially irritating to the gastric lining. But don't forget that even buffered aspirin can cause stomach irritation through the indirect route of prostaglandin inhibition.

Q. My aunt always takes her aspirin with a big glass of water. Does that make sense?

A. You bet! Taking aspirin with a glass of water is part of an age-old tradition. As long ago as 1899 a German physician told his patients that "aspirin should not be swallowed whole but allowed to disintegrate in a little sugar water flavored with two drops of lemon juice."[4] Our modern-day recommendation would be to drop two aspirin tablets in a glass of sparkling mineral water and allow them to dissolve first.

Another option was suggested in the pages of the *Journal of the American Medical Association*: the tablets should be "thoroughly chewed and swallowed with an adequate amount of water or they should be crushed to a fine powder and the powder taken as a suspension in orange juice."[5] Instead of orange juice, we suggest a non-acidic beverage. And for those in a hurry, two pills washed down with a full 8-ounce glass of water is still a time-honored way of taking aspirin.

Q. So do you need to crush the aspirin, too?

A. We have found the crush method inconvenient and messy. It is hard to get crushed-up regular aspirin to dissolve in water. Chewing the aspirin, then drinking the water is a little easier, but you have to make sure you rinse your mouth well so there is no aspirin residue left on your gums. Any little pieces that get left could cause irritation. To be honest, aspirin doesn't taste too hot either.

Q. Why not just take a couple of Alka-Seltzers?

A. That's not a bad solution, although it's a lot more expensive than generic aspirin. Each effervescent **Alka-Seltzer** tablet contains the equivalent of one regular-strength aspirin. There are two advantages to **Alka-Seltzer**. First, the aspirin is already dissolved before it hits your stomach, so there is less risk of direct irritation. Second, the antacid (sodium bicarbonate—or baking soda) provides extra neutralizing action that may speed absorption and diminish the risk of stomach bleeding.

So **Alka-Seltzer** sounds terrific, right? Yes and no. There are several drawbacks to this formulation, besides the hefty price. The buffering agent, sodium bicarbonate, can cause alkalinization of the urine. This speeds elimination of salicylate from the body and means you might get less bang for your buck. In other words, the baking soda component may reduce salicylate effectiveness. Even more important, **Alka-Seltzer** contains a whopping dose of sodium (567 mg per tablet). For people on salt-restricted diets, regular use of **Alka-Seltzer** would be a major no-no!

Q. And how about aspirin in powder form?

A. This is quite popular in the South. The two classic brands in North Carolina are **BC Powder** and **Goody's Headache Powder**. Both products contain aspirin that is readily dissolved in water. The problem is that they also contain other pain relievers. And in most cases we tend to shy away from combination analgesics. We only wish there were a pure aspirin powder that was readily available and inexpensive. If such a product existed, it would be our number one aspirin choice!

Q. That brings us to, well, the end of the line.

A. Yes, and in the United States this is probably the least popular method of all. A final way to bypass the stomach altogether is to take your aspirin in suppository form. There are a number of generic house brands on the market as well as products from large manufacturers like Lilly, which sells **A.S.A.** Please remember to remove the foil cover before inserting any suppository. You'd be surprised how many pharmacists chuckle about complaints of irritation from the foil wrapper. Although suppositories are unpopular in the U.S., they are big sellers in France.

Q. And how about liquid aspirin?

A. To get an aspirinlike drug in liquid form (besides aspirin powders or **Alka-Seltzer**), you will have to go to one of aspirin's kissing cousins (see Chapter 20). Instead of acetylsalicylic acid (aspirin), you could try choline salicylate (**Arthropan**). It is available in liquid form and is especially helpful for those who have trouble swallowing pills. Unfortunately, choline salicylate is less effective at easing pain or lowering fever than aspirin, though it will relieve inflammation for arthritis victims. To obtain an equivalent effect, you have to swallow 435 mg of **Arthropan** for each 325 mg of aspirin. **Arthropan** is available without a prescription.

Q. So any final words on trying to take aspirin without irritating your stomach?

A. It will take trial and error. Every person is different. If you are one of those people with a sensitive stomach, you should seek the advice and collaboration of a trusted health professional.

Q. I take aspirin regularly and have never had any stomach upset. But I have recently increased my dose and am worried about ulcers. How much aspirin can I safely take without hurting my stomach?

A. There is no way to predict how much aspirin will cause any particular person problems. Some people can take as many as ten or more pills daily and not experience stomach upset. Others find that as little as one pill every other day can cause them distress. Listening to your body is about the best advice we can offer. Symptoms of serious GI problems include chronic indigestion, heartburn, nausea, and stomach pain. And stay alert for signs of a "silent" ulcer. Report anything unusual to your physician immediately.

Q. Can you have an aspirin-caused ulcer without having any pain symptoms?

A. Ulcers can sometimes occur without early warning signs of trouble. If you are taking high doses of aspirin regularly, stay in close touch with your doctor and pay attention to your body. Report any symptoms such as chronic heartburn, loss of weight, fatigue, and lethargy. If you feel full before you have eaten your usual helping, that can be a sign of trouble. Go in for periodic blood tests to make sure you are not becoming anemic.

Q. I had ulcers 20 years ago. No problems since. Can I take aspirin now?

A. The standard recommendation is to avoid aspirin if you are prone to ulcers. But given that your problem occurred 20 years ago, you may be able to get away with small doses under a doctor's supervision.

Q. I have a strong family history of stomach ulcers, although to date I have had no trouble myself. I want to

take aspirin as a preventive for heart disease, stroke, and colon cancer. What should I do?

A. As always, check with your physician first. We can't say with certainty that some people inherit a high risk of ulcers or if there are other factors at work. Certainly your family history should make you cautious, but not paranoid.

Probably more important than your genes is the dose of aspirin you take. The lower the dose, the better your chances of avoiding problems. (But remember, there are no guarantees of 100 percent safety.) Ask your physician if he thinks you can get by with one baby aspirin daily or even every other day. That may provide the protection you seek at an acceptable risk. One recent study showed that as little as one aspirin pill a week could cut the chances of coming down with colon cancer by 50 percent.[6] At that dose your chances of developing tummy trouble are lower.

Q. I don't exactly experience stomach irritation after taking aspirin, but I do frequently feel a tiny bit of nausea. Could this be a sign of an ulcer?

A. Symptoms of an ulcer can vary tremendously from one individual to another. Pain is the most common sign that all is not well. Some people describe it as a gnawing pain, while others describe the discomfort as burning or aching. Many people do not experience any pain at all.

Nausea could conceivably be a symptom of an ulcer, but it is not as common as pain. You may just be sensitive to aspirin. Some people experience nausea and vomiting because of stomach irritation. Another explanation is that aspirin affects the chemoreceptor trigger zone, or CTZ, in your brain. When this part of your brain is stimulated, nausea is a common reaction. This usually only occurs after high doses (ten or more pills daily). But it may occur at lower levels in those who are especially sensitive. Please check in with your doctor so he or she knows about the nausea and can take appropriate action.

Q. Is taking aspirin with milk enough to prevent bleeding or stomach upset?

A. You could drink a gallon of milk with each aspirin pill and it still would not guarantee complete protection. Milk offers some protection against the direct irritating effects of aspirin. But milk cannot prevent the secondary toxic effect on the stomach.

Q. I take high-dose aspirin regularly and have never had any stomach pain, but I worry about the kind of damage that may be occurring without my knowing it. Can you fill me in on this?

A. Your concerns are justified. Some people never experience any indigestion or feel any pain and yet can have severe damage to the stomach lining after high-dose aspirin. The only way for a physician to really know what is going on in the digestive tract is to look. That means endoscopy, in which a tube is stuck down your throat so the doctor can actually look for irritation or ulcers. Since endoscopy is not one of the more delightful experiences in life, many people try to avoid this procedure. You will have to check with your physician to see if it is necessary in your case.

Q. Regular aspirin bothers my stomach, but I have discovered that the identical dose of baby aspirin does not. Perhaps this will be useful to your other readers.

A. We're glad that you have found a trick to escape stomach upset. We know of no studies that have actually looked at the issue of baby aspirin and stomach upset. It may be that baby aspirin are easier to chew, and chewing your aspirin does the trick. Or perhaps baby aspirin pills dissolve more readily than regular aspirin. The only downside to your recommendation is that baby aspirin (or low-dose adult aspirin) is much more expensive.

Q. I am currently using Ascriptin. Please tell me about the various forms of aspirin I can take to avoid stomach upset.

A. Ascriptin is nothing more than aspirin with antacids. Each **Ascriptin** contains 325 mg of aspirin along with 50 mg of magnesium hydroxide, 50 mg of aluminum hydroxide, and 50 mg of calcium carbonate. **Ascriptin Extra Strength** has 500 mg of aspirin with 80 mg each of the same three antacids.

You could get the same purported benefits from taking aspirin simultaneously with antacids, but it is more convenient to swallow the whole thing in one pill. There are a number of other formulations that attempt to do much the same thing. **Extra Strength Tri-Buffered Bufferin**, for example, contains 500 mg of aspirin with 222.3 mg of calcium carbonate, 88.9 mg of magnesium oxide, and 55.6 mg of magnesium carbonate. And **Cama Arthritis Pain Reliever** has 500 mg of aspirin with 150 mg of magnesium oxide and 150 mg of aluminum hydroxide. Buffered aspirin is also available inexpensively in generic house brands.

Another option is enteric coated aspirin. It seems to help some people with sensitive stomachs. It is designed to dissolve in the small intestine instead of the stomach. **Ecotrin** is the most popular brand, but many pharmacies carry a much cheaper house brand. **A.S.A. Enseals** is also coated and contains the equivalent of two tablets in one (650 mg of aspirin). **Easprin** (prescription only) has 975 mg of aspirin in each coated tablet.

A third option would be aspirin suppositories. This is a little messier and generally less popular with Americans than with people in other countries. It is, however, one way to bypass the stomach and reduce direct irritation.

A caution is in order with all these products, whether they be aspirin with antacids, liquid aspirin, or coated aspirin. None is a surefire guarantee of avoiding stomach upset. Aspirin has an indirect effect on the stomach lining so that it can cause upset and ulceration even when taken as a suppository or administered intravenously.

□　　□　　□　　□

References

1. Dolan, Carrie. "What Soothes Aches, Makes Flowers Last, And Grows Hair?" *Wall Street Journal*, Feb. 19, 1988, p. 1.
2. Fries, James F. "NSAID Gastropathy: Epidemiology." *J. Musculoskel. Med.* 1991; 8(2):21–28.
3. Paulus, H.E. "FDA Arthritis Advisory Committee Meeting: Post-Marketing Surveillance of Non-Steroidal Anti-Inflammatory Drugs." *Arthritis Rheum.* 1985; 28:1168–1169.
4. Collier, H.O.J. "Aspirin." *Scientific American* 1963; 209:97–108.
5. Blaker, Martin I. "Crushed Aspirin Tablets." *JAMA* 1974; 230:1385.
6. "Aspirin Cuts Cancer Risk." *Medical Tribune* 1992; 33(21):1.

CHAPTER 12

ASPIRIN AND YOUR BLOOD

Aspirin has a profound effect on blood. As little as 30 mg (less than one tenth of a standard pill) can prevent platelets from clumping together. This leads to increased bleeding time and a reduced risk of stroke or heart attack. Interestingly, other formulations of salicylate (kissing cousins of aspirin) do not possess this effect. That means that products like **Original Doan's** pills (magnesium salicylate), **Arthropan** (choline salicylate), and **Uracel 5** (sodium salicylate) won't reduce the risk of blood clots, but also shouldn't increase the likelihood of bruising or bleeding.

Because aspirin "thins the blood," it should not be used by anyone with a bleeding disorder or a tendency to bleed. That means anyone with hemophilia, bleeding ulcers, or hemorrhage. A history of hemorrhagic stroke would be a contraindication to aspirin use. Someone taking other anticoagulants (**Coumadin** or heparin) should avoid aspirin unless there is careful medical supervision in a hospital setting. People who have undergone a tonsillectomy or other surgery should avoid aspirin for at least a week unless a physician has advised otherwise.

❑   ❑   ❑   ❑

Q. I am planning to have hemorrhoid surgery next month. A friend who has been through this warned me

that I must plan to discontinue my regular aspirin use before and after I am in the hospital, because it might cause bleeding. Is this true? If so, how long will I have to abstain? Why hasn't my doctor mentioned anything about this?

A. Aspirin definitely affects bleeding. Our drug bible (*Goodman and Gilman's The Pharmacological Basis of Therapeutics*) says that a standard dose of 650 mg can double the average bleeding time, and this effect lasts from four to seven days. The recommendation is made that "if conditions permit, aspirin therapy should be stopped at least one week prior to surgery."[1] In some situations this suggestion may have to be modified, so please check with your surgeon well in advance of the operation to get his advice on this critical issue. You will likely have to wait at least one week after the surgery before resuming aspirin use.

Q. How much aspirin may I take before it thins the blood?

A. Aspirin can alter the sticky part of blood (platelets) at extremely small doses. Bleeding time is substantially increased with a single baby aspirin (81 mg). It is entirely possible that half this dose would also have a measurable effect. The point is that almost any aspirin dose will affect the ability of blood to clot.

Q. After taking an aspirin a day for about a year, I noticed that I would bleed profusely whenever I cut myself. I cut back to one tablet every other day and have seen some improvement, but I wonder if, at age 67, I would be better off if my blood were thinner.

A. No one knows the optimal dose of aspirin or the ideal "thinness" of blood. Older people may need to be especially careful about the dose if they bruise too easily.

Some people appear more vulnerable than others when it comes to aspirin. If after a minor cut you bleed for what seems like a long time (in a special research setting that would be 11 minutes), you may be what researchers call a hyper responder.[2] This means you may be more vulnerable to hemorrhage or a bleeding stroke.

Anyone who bleeds profusely or bruises easily after a minor bump should check in with a physician for testing and evaluation.

Q. My mother takes an aspirin a day for "thick blood" (sticky platelets). Does this run in families? Should I be taking aspirin too?

A. Platelets are the part of blood that clumps together to form clots that stop bleeding. If your mother is at risk of a blood clot, then aspirin may well be appropriate for her. The information you have provided is not enough to determine whether you are also at risk. You would need to have some blood tests done to determine your bleeding time. Your physician can perform these tests and advise you on whether aspirin use would be appropriate.

Q. I had a bout with bleeding problems about a year ago, but switched to buffered aspirin and have had no problems since. Is buffered aspirin less likely to cause bleeding problems than the regular variety?

A. Buffered aspirin is identical to regular aspirin in all respects. The only difference is that one or more antacids are added to the tablet. This shouldn't affect aspirin's potential for causing bleeding problems. So you shouldn't assume that buffered aspirin is safer.

Q. I stopped taking aspirin because I get nosebleeds. Do you think I should take it again?

A. Aspirin may increase the risk of nosebleeds in susceptible people. This drug may also make it harder to get a nosebleed to stop. Unless there is a clear medical reason for you to take aspirin (with your doctor's supervision, of course), we would encourage you to lay off.

Q. I have heavy menstrual flow from 24 to 60 hours after it begins each month. I attribute this to the aspirin I take (four or five Easprin tablets daily) for osteoarthritis. Each is the equivalent of several aspirin tablets. Can this be so? Also I am very lethargic. Could heavy use of aspirin cause this? They've tested me for everything and found nothing wrong.

A. Have they tested you for anemia? People who take large doses of aspirin for arthritis often bleed from their stomach and develop anemia. When you add a heavy menstrual flow to the blood loss caused by stomach irritation, the possibility of anemia is magnified.

Q. I take a lot of aspirin (two to three Anacin four times per day) and worry that this may be too much. While I haven't noticed any prolonged bleeding when I get a cut, I do bruise much more easily—I have multiple bruises all over my body at the moment. Surprisingly, I don't have any problems with my stomach.

A. Bruising is one sign of aspirin's effect on blood. Some people can be more susceptible to this adverse reaction than others. Ask your doctor if it would be worthwhile to test your bleeding time. If you are a hyper responder (someone who bleeds longer after aspirin than normal), you may have to cut back or eliminate aspirin entirely.

Q. On two separate occasions, two years apart, I started taking one aspirin daily. Both times, after about a month, I noticed bruiselike black marks on my hands and arms. It appeared that the small blood vessels under the skin were "leaking." The slightest pressure, such as someone taking my hand, would cause these broken blood vessels. I believe in the therapeutic value of aspirin and wonder if a smaller dose might be the answer. I would appreciate your suggestions as to the cause and solution to this problem.

A. A smaller dose is not likely to help. One study found that even a dose as low as 74 mg (less than a baby aspirin) could prolong bleeding time significantly. You may be supersensitive to aspirin. Some people bleed far longer than others, and this may increase their risk of hemorrhage. Given your situation, we'd recommend that you not take aspirin without a doctor's very careful supervision.

Q. What is an aspirin hyper responder?

A. Researchers have identified a subgroup of individuals they call hyper responders, or HRs for short.[3] These individuals are perfectly healthy, but react to even small doses of aspirin with prolonged bleeding times.

In special tests, people will bleed for about 5 minutes after a tiny incision. If they take aspirin, the bleeding time goes up to about 7 minutes (measured 4 to 12 hours after aspirin ingestion). Hyper responders may bleed for 10 to 20 minutes after a single small dose of aspirin. Although this research is quite preliminary, it has led investigators to speculate that HRs could be people who are more susceptible to bruising or hemorrhagic strokes. If proven, then HRs may have to forego aspirin except under careful medical supervision.

❏   ❏   ❏   ❏

References

1. Gilman, Alfred G., et al., eds. *Goodman and Gilman's The Pharmacological Basis of Therapeutics, 8th ed.* New York: Pergamon Press, 1990, pp. 647–648.
2. Fiore, Louis D., et al. "The Bleeding Time Response to Aspirin." *Am. J. Clin. Pathol.* 1990; 94:292–296.
3. Ibid.

CHAPTER 13

OTHER SIDE EFFECTS OF ASPIRIN

Aspirin can do other unpleasant things to your body besides make you bleed and give you a stomachache. Although a rare complication, aspirin can make kidney disease worse. High doses may cause visual problems, thirst, fever, and headache, and can do bad things to your liver. An unexplained itchy rash could be brought on by aspirin, even in low doses. People with asthma can be especially susceptible to runny nose, nasal polyps (grapelike growths), and breathing problems. This can be a tricky side effect because it may come on slowly, hours after taking aspirin. Some asthmatics have not realized that their worsening condition was aspirin-induced. But perhaps the most common of all these additional complications is tinnitus, or ringing in the ears. This aspirin side effect can signal hearing damage and always calls for a medical consultation. Tinnitus is usually a sign that you have reached the upper limit of aspirin dosing and must cut back till the ringing disappears.

❑　　❑　　❑　　❑

Q. I am very concerned about continued ringing in the ears and a possible permanent hearing loss that may

have been caused by aspirin. How can aspirin affect your hearing and how can I avoid future problems?

A. You have identified one of the more serious complications of aspirin. Ringing in the ears (tinnitus) is usually associated with high doses, but some people are especially vulnerable and can experience hearing problems at so-called normal amounts. These symptoms are thought to be brought on either by increased pressure within the ear canal or by a toxic effect on tiny hair cells that are critical for hearing.

These side effects are usually reversible when the drug is stopped. But if toxic doses are taken for long periods of time, there may be some lasting consequences. Check with an ear, nose, and throat specialist for complete evaluation.

Q. Can aspirin cause light-headedness? Blindness?

A. Aspirin can cause dizziness, fatigue, mental confusion, dimness of vision, and irritability, but usually only after very high doses. We know of no studies to suggest that blindness would be caused by standard aspirin doses.

Q. Is there any reason to cancel surgery because I took aspirin a week before entering the hospital?

A. As long as one full week (seven days) has elapsed after your last dose before surgery, there should be little difficulty. Better check with the surgeon, though, just to be on the safe side.

Q. My husband has been taking an aspirin a day for many years. I am worried that the drug will build up in his body to the level where it causes harmful side effects. Is there any risk of this?

A. Aspirin does not accumulate in the body the way some long-acting medicines can. But even at this low level there are risks. Stomach upset, bleeding, and ulceration are always possible. That is why it is important for your husband to check in with his physician periodically for a review of his aspirin program. If he has kidney disease, aspirin might be a special problem.

Q. My 13-year-old son recently had a headache and I gave him aspirin. Within an hour he had developed a rash on his neck. Over the next two weeks it spread down his trunk and itched like crazy. I suspect this is an aspirin allergy. Our pediatrician says this type of reaction is very rare. Do you think it could be an allergy?

A. Aspirin allergy is not that rare. It can show up as a rash, hives, breathing difficulty, wheezing, runny nose, and nasal polyps. People with a history of asthma or hives may be especially susceptible. In rare cases life-threatening anaphylactic shock can occur.

Your son's reaction sounds suspiciously like aspirin allergy. He will probably have to avoid aspirin in all forms for the rest of his life. Other NSAIDs (nonsteroidal antiinflammatory drugs) could be a problem for him as well.

Q. At my recent annual physical, my doctor detected the presence of blood in my stool. Could this be due to the high doses of aspirin I take for my arthritis?

A. It's a distinct possibility. People who must take large doses of aspirin (12 to 14 pills daily) lose anywhere from 3 to 8 ml (milliliters) of blood through their stool.

Q. I have been taking high-dose aspirin for my arthritis for three or four years now, and lately my nails have been splitting and breaking something awful. When I stopped aspirin for three weeks, my nails seemed to improve. Is there a connection between aspirin and brittle nails?

A. We could find no reference to nail problems and aspirin. This one is a mystery to us. Arthritis itself can sometimes affect the nail bed, so it may not be the aspirin after all.

Fungal infections of the nails can also produce the symptoms you describe.

Q. Does aspirin have any effect on blood pressure?

A. In most cases, aspirin shouldn't have a significant effect on blood pressure. One study did show that three tablets daily raised systolic pressure up to 2 points and diastolic blood pressure about 1/2 point.[1] And some individuals may have unusual reactions to aspirin. If you suspect that aspirin is raising your blood pressure, it would be a simple matter to get a home blood pressure cuff and check your pressure before starting on aspirin and periodically thereafter to determine if there is any noticeable difference.

People who take blood pressure medicines like **Inderal** (propranolol) or **Visken** (pindolol) may discover that these drugs don't work as well as expected if they also take aspirin. Blood pressure may rise because of this kind of combination. Other beta blocker drugs (**Blocadren, Corgard, Kerlone, Lopressor, Sectral, Tenormin**) might also be affected, so if you are taking one, please have your blood pressure monitored routinely.

Although there isn't much data on other drugs, concern has been raised that aspirin might alter the antihypertensive impact of popular medications like **Vasotec** (enalapril) or **Capoten** (captopril).

Q. Fifteen years ago, I was told I was allergic to aspirin and should never take it again, but with the news of aspirin's preventive effects, I would like to give it a try, if I could do so safely. Is aspirin allergy irreversible? How common is it? Is there any way to reverse it?

A. Please do not give aspirin a try on your own. Aspirin allergy can produce mild symptoms, such as a rash, hives, and runny nose, or it could provoke an asthma attack, severe breathing problems, and life-threatening shock. Even a small dose could cause you distress. Aspirin allergy is not uncommon, especially in people who have a history of hives or asthma.

It is unclear whether you can reverse aspirin allergy. There are reports of "desensitization" done in a hospital under careful medical supervision. Once accomplished, it may be possible to maintain desensitization by taking one aspirin daily.[2] This is not a do-it-yourself project. Check with an expert allergist before even considering such a program. Unsupervised experimentation could cost you your life.

Q. Can taking large doses of aspirin every day affect my sex life?

A. There are no studies that might shed light on this important question. As far as we know, aspirin has no direct effect on sexuality, either positively or negatively. There is one way aspirin may have an indirectly beneficial impact. When you hear the refrain, "Not tonight, dear, I have a headache," you could always reach for the aspirin bottle. Then again, you could always plan ahead and suggest a little aspirin after dinner to prevent a headache before the fireworks start.

Aspirin may have another, more important role in sexuality. There is clear correlation between atherosclerosis, or clogged coronary arteries, and arterial obstruction in the penis. This could lead to difficulties in filling the penis with blood so that it can become erect. There is a remote possibility that aspirin may also help protect against vascular problems in this important organ. At the very least, aspirin can prevent heart attacks and strokes and therefore help protect people against conditions that would impair sexual fulfillment.

Dr. Theresa Crenshaw, the country's leading expert on sexual pharmacology, offers one caution: "Both aspirin and ibuprofen decrease pain by inhibiting prostaglandins. Prostaglandins can be successfully used to produce erection through injection in males. Because prostaglandins naturally induce pain, prostaglandin inhibitors work by acting on these substances. On the one hand, aspirin complements erections in the same way that it protects against stroke. On the other hand, it inhibits prostaglandins, which may directly inhibit erection.''[3]

There is no data that suggest aspirin actually does impair or prevent erections. But Dr. Crenshaw is absolutely right that doctors do inject the prostaglandin PGE_2 directly into the penis to produce erections. Since aspirin can block the manufacture of PGE_2 in the body, it is conceivable that less of this important substance might pose a problem for some men. Given the number of men taking aspirin, it would be nice to have an answer to this intriguing question.

If you suspect aspirin is interfering with your love life, check with your doctor to see if he can devise an experiment to test this hypothesis.

Q. After 30 years taking Anacin, I developed a sneezing allergy which always occurs within 90 minutes of taking one or two tablets. I have the same reaction to Bufferin and Bayer. I had to give up aspirin and switch to Tylenol. Is there any way to counteract or reverse this effect?

A. It doesn't matter how you take your aspirin—buffered, brand name, or in a different form such as in **Aspergum** or **Alka-Seltzer**. The runny nose and sneezing are likely brought on by aspirin allergy.

Desensitization is possible but only under an allergist's careful supervision and preferably in a hospital. It might be easier, safer, and cheaper to give up aspirin and stick with acetaminophen (**Tylenol**).

Q. Can I take aspirin safely if I have chronic bronchial asthma?

A. This is a sticky wicket. As many as one in five asthma patients may be hypersensitive to aspirin. Their immune systems react strangely. For one thing, they may develop growths (polyps) in the nose. More serious are asthma attacks that can include wheezing, swelling in the neck, and severe breathing difficulties. These symptoms may come on within a few minutes or may be delayed up to several hours or longer. Rash, hives, and runny nose are other possible complications of aspirin.

If you have never experienced any such symptoms after taking aspirin, you may not be vulnerable. If you have never taken aspirin and don't know if you are sensitive, we would encourage you to undertake testing only in a doctor's office or in a hospital.

Q. I am very concerned about Reye's syndrome. What is the current scientific thinking regarding this disease and its relation to the salicylates?

A. There is no longer much doubt that aspirin is somehow connected with Reye's syndrome. Children and teenagers who have either influenza or chicken pox must avoid aspirin or salicylates in any form (including **Pepto-Bismol, Aspergum,** and **Alka-Seltzer**).

Epidemiologist Devra Lee Davis and her colleague Patricia Buffler have calculated that during the five years (1981 to 1986) the Food and Drug Administration debated adding a warning label about Reye's to aspirin containers, 1,470 excess deaths may have occurred.[4] Once the warning label about Reye's syndrome was placed on aspirin bottles, the incidence of this potentially deadly disease dropped dramatically.

Q. What are the ages when aspirin is dangerous in Reye's syndrome? Is it a problem for older teenagers or adults?

A. The recommendation is for children and teenagers (until they reach the age of 20) to avoid aspirin if the flu or chicken pox is suspected. There is no reason to believe that adults are more susceptible to this rare condition if they take aspirin.

Q. I have had asthma for some time now and would like to take aspirin but have been afraid. Can you provide me with guidelines for taking aspirin safely even though I have asthma?

A. There is no safe way for you to take aspirin if you are asthmatic and are also sensitive to aspirin. (Roughly 4 to 19 percent of asthmatics are hypersensitive to aspirin.) If you have never had any symptoms of aspirin allergy (rash, breathing difficulties, nasal polyps, or a worsening of the asthma) you may be able to tolerate aspirin, but only under a doctor's supervision.

Q. A young neighbor of ours recently developed severe physical problems and a profound learning disability. Rumor has it that she was running a high fever and was given aspirin. Can you make any sense of this?

A. One possible explanation is that she experienced a case of Reye's syndrome and was left with some residual brain damage. Of course, there are any number of other possibilities. Only her physician can clear up the mystery.

Q. Does a residue of aspirin remain in the body? If it does, how long does it last? Is this a problem one should consider in deciding about aspirin use?

A. Aspirin is absorbed very quickly from the digestive tract. Within 30 minutes there are substantial amounts in the bloodstream. The peak effect occurs after about two hours and then gradually wears off over the next several hours.

Aspirin is quickly converted to a number of breakdown products (metabolites) such as salicylic acid, salicylate, and salicyluric acid. Most salicylate will have disappeared from the body within 4 to 12 hours. After high doses, a day or two may be necessary for aspirin metabolites to be eliminated. Aspirin's effect on blood cells like platelets may last

as long as a week, but the aspirin itself should be long gone
from the body.

**Q. Can long-term use of high-dose aspirin cause
diarrhea?**

A. Aspirin can affect the digestive tract in a number of
unpleasant ways. Indigestion, nausea, vomiting, and diarrhea are all possibilities.

**Q. Does aspirin have any effect on urination? It seems
to me I urinate less when I take it, but this could be just
my imagination.**

A. Fluid retention is one side effect of aspirin. That could
mean that you might urinate a little less after a standard
dose. This should not pose a problem under most circum-
stances, but people with heart failure or kidney problems
might put themselves at greater risk if they take large doses.

**Q. I am frequently bothered by constipation after taking
aspirin. Is this my imagination or is it a real side effect?**

A. Although it is not a common side effect, constipation
could be one complication of regular use.

**Q. I am 90 years old. I started taking one aspirin a day at
my doctor's suggestion for about a year and a half. Then
one day I discovered that I could not hear my daughter
talk, I just saw her lips move. My doctor could not believe
that aspirin was the cause. He wanted me to see an ear
doctor. I stopped the aspirin and in a week my hearing
came back. My doctor put me on a baby aspirin and so
far everything has been okay.**

A. Aspirin can definitely cause hearing loss, though rarely
at so low a dose. That your hearing came back after dis-
continuing aspirin strongly suggests that this was a drug-
induced effect.

Because you are so sensitive to this complication, we

would encourage you to have a hearing test to make sure you are not experiencing a gradual deterioration even at the mini-dose you are currently taking.

Q. Can a person become addicted to aspirin?

A. *Addiction* is a term that drives us crazy because it carries such emotional baggage and is so unspecific. If what you mean is, Can you become physically dependent on aspirin and suffer withdrawal upon sudden discontinuation? the answer is a firm *no*!

If by addiction you mean, Can someone become psychologically addicted? the answer is yes. We have known people who swallowed a dozen or more pills daily. They didn't suffer pain or any other ailment but felt compelled to swallow aspirin just as some people feel compelled to eat jelly beans or potato chips or drink glass after glass of water. The point is that people can become psychologically dependent on just about anything, including aspirin.

Q. Does frequent use of aspirin lessen the beneficial effects?

A. This is a more complex question than most physicians would ever imagine. The textbook answer is no. Theoretically, people can take large aspirin doses daily without experiencing any reduction in benefit.

And yet we have talked to many people who swear that the benefits of aspirin do diminish over time. They insist that if they take a "drug holiday" (without any aspirin) for a week or so, they can reestablish aspirin's pain-relieving power. We have never seen any research to back up these anecdotal claims, but we tend to believe that some people with arthritis may indeed develop a kind of tolerance to the pain-relieving effects of anti-inflammatory drugs.

❏   ❏   ❏   ❏

References

1. Aspirin Myocardial Infarction Study Research Group: A Randomized Controlled Trial of Aspirin in Persons Recovered from Myocardial Infarction." *JAMA* 1980; 243:661–669.
2. Olin, Bernie R., et al., eds. *Drug Facts and Comparisons*. St. Louis: Facts and Comparisons, 1992.
3. Crenshaw, Theresa L. *Beyond Aphrodisiacs*. New York: Norton.
4. Davis, Devra Lee and Buffler, Patricia. "Reduction of Deaths After Drug Labelling for Risk of Reye's Syndrome." *Lancet* 1992: 340:1042.

CHAPTER 14

DRUGS AND FOODS THAT INTERACT WITH ASPIRIN

Aspirin is one of those drugs that people tend to take for granted. When you take one little pill every day for weeks, months, or years, you almost forget that it's a drug. Just as women who take birth control pills can forget that they are taking medicine, someone who pops down a baby aspirin may fail to mention to the doctor that he or she takes a medication daily. That could be a serious error.

Aspirin, even in small doses, can interact with a surprising number of other drugs. Certain blood pressure medicines may be affected by aspirin. Other arthritis drugs can become far more dangerous in combination with aspirin. And people who like to head off a hangover by popping down aspirin after a night on the town can cause serious damage to their digestive tracts. For a complete table of aspirin interactions, turn to Appendix III at the end of this book.

❑   ❑   ❑   ❑

Q. My girlfriend always takes aspirin before a party because she's convinced this will help her get more alcohol into her bloodstream more quickly. Is she right about

this? Is taking aspirin before a party a good idea? What about preventing a headache?

A. Your girlfriend may well be technically correct, but she could also be making a big mistake. A recent study suggests that aspirin could increase blood alcohol levels when taken before drinking.[1] The authors of the work conclude that while the increase in blood alcohol levels after taking aspirin "is small, it can be of clinical significance for individuals driving cars or operating other machinery that requires a high degree of mental and motor coordination."[2] We don't recommend this strategy. People who insist on popping aspirin prior to partying should be extremely careful.

Taking aspirin after alcohol also poses problems. Booze, wine, beer, or any other form of alcohol can dissolve away the protective mucus coating in the stomach. This makes your tender tummy far more susceptible to aspirin irritation. It is likely to bleed and bleed. For this reason we discourage people from taking aspirin to prevent a hangover.

Q. I have heard that if you take aspirin with foods containing vitamin C, one or the other is canceled out. Is this true? If so, which one?

A. There is some data suggesting that aspirin may partially prevent the passage of vitamin C into cells, especially platelets and white blood cells.[3] Aspirin may also speed elimination of vitamin C from the body through the kidneys. Although it is unclear what this means, some researchers have suggested that patients who take large doses of aspirin for arthritis may need extra vitamin C. Older people may be especially vulnerable to low levels of vitamin C. An ascorbic acid supplement may also be a good idea for someone taking standard doses of aspirin on a regular basis.

Q. Should I take aspirin with food, or does it work more quickly without?

A. Food can diminish the direct irritating effects of aspirin on the stomach lining. That is why many doctors tell patients to take aspirin or other arthritis medicine at mealtime. Food does delay absorption, however, and may thus slightly slow pain relief.

Q. What foods contain aspirin? Tea? Broccoli? What else?

A. While food doesn't actually contain pure aspirin (acetylsalicylic acid) per se, many diverse foods do contain salicylate, one of the main breakdown products of aspirin. Prunes, raisins, raspberries, licorice, curry powder, paprika, tea, pickles, worcestershire sauce, oregano, dill, and mustard are just a few foods that contain substantial quantities of salicylate (over 5 mg per 100 g of food). Broccoli has a more modest salicylate content, under 1 mg per 100 g. On average, Americans take in anywhere from 10 to 200 mg of salicylate daily from food. This is nothing to worry about, but if you are allergic to aspirin, you may also be allergic to salicylates and those foods could cause you some trouble.

Q. Is it safe to take aspirin with other pain-killing drugs?

A. That depends upon the other pain killers. Concern has been raised about combining aspirin with over-the-counter analgesics like acetaminophen (**Anacin-3, APAP, Goody's Headache Powder, Panadol, Tylenol**, etc.) or salicylamide (**BC Powder, DeWitt Pills, Presalin, Rid-A-Pain, S-A-C, Tri-Pain Caplets, Valesin**, etc.). The worry is that prolonged use of aspirin with these drugs may increase the risk of kidney damage.[4] This risk has not been firmly established, but we encourage you to discuss this issue with your physician to see if it could be a problem for you.

Q. How about Empirin with codeine? Is this safe?

A. Empirin with codeine and other aspirin-codeine combinations are a good choice for short-term situations in which you may need more analgesic power than aspirin alone can provide (e.g., a bad toothache or a back spasm). Aspirin-codeine combinations are available by prescription only. They appear to be quite safe, and can provide high-powered pain relief, but you wouldn't want to rely on codeine for too long, though, as it could lead to dependence.

Q. Since I started taking aspirin, I have noticed that my athlete's foot remedy (tolnaftate) seems "hotter" and much more effective. Could the mildly acid excretion inhibit fungus growth?

A. This makes no sense to us, pharmacologically, but if you think you get better results, great!

Q. When I was in the hospital, I was given Motrin and aspirin together. Is it safe to take this combination?

A. Ibuprofen and aspirin work through a similar mechanism, so it is hard for us to imagine that they would provide significantly better pain relief together than either alone. The risk of stomach upset or ulceration would be magnified by taking both drugs simultaneously. While you could probably get by with this combination while under close medical supervision in the hospital, we would not recommend such a regimen on your own.

Q. Can aspirin interfere with my high blood pressure pills?

A. It just might, especially if you are taking blood pressure medicines like **Inderal** (propranolol) or **Visken** (pindolol). Blood pressure may rise because of this kind of combination. Other beta blocker drugs (**Blocadren, Corgard, Kerlone, Lopressor, Sectral, Tenormin**) might also be affected, so if you are taking one, please have your blood pressured monitored routinely.

Q. I am an 84-year-old man who had a heart attack two years ago. I am on Coumadin, Cardene, and Tenoretic. Recently I developed a constant pain from osteoarthritis.

Would it make sense to switch from Coumadin to aspirin and get the double benefit of blood thinning and pain relief?

A. What an interesting concept, but first a caution. DO NOT EVER mix **Coumadin** (warfarin) and aspirin. The two drugs together could lead to fatal hemorrhaging.

Coumadin is prescribed to prevent blood clots. People who have experienced thrombophlebitis, pulmonary embolisms, atrial fibrillation, or heart attacks are often prescribed this anticoagulant. It works differently from aspirin to prolong bleeding time and prevent blood clots. **Coumadin** blocks vitamin K, an essential clotting factor. Bleeding time (prothrombin time) is prolonged, and hemorrhage is a constant worry for people taking this medicine. Aspirin can also increase the risk of hemorrhaging but does so by making the sticky part of blood (platelets) less likely to clump together and form clots.

There is certainly ample evidence that aspirin can prevent blood clots. It reduces the risk of second heart attacks and strokes. New analysis of the Physicians' Health Study shows it can also help diminish the need for surgery associated with circulatory problems. But whether aspirin can sometimes be used as a substitute for **Coumadin** remains unresolved. This decision can only be made by your physician.

❑ ❑ ❑ ❑

References

1. Roine, Risto, et al. "Aspirin Increases Blood Alcohol Concentrations in Humans After Ingestion of Ethanol." *JAMA* 1990; 264:2406–2408.
2. Ibid.
3. Roe, Daphne A. *Drug-Induced Nutritional Deficiencies.* Westport: Avi Publishing Co., 1976.
4. Clive, D.M., and Stoff, J.S. "Renal Syndromes Associated with Nonsteroidal Anti-inflammatory Drugs." *N. Engl. J. Med.* 1984; 310:563–572.

CHAPTER 15

PREVENTING ASPIRIN OVERDOSE: HOW MUCH IS TOO MUCH?

Most people assume they will never experience aspirin overdose. That may not be a safe assumption. Imagine someone who is taking aspirin for arthritis or a really bad headache. It would not be unusual to swallow two or three pills every three or four hours all day long. By the evening that could add up to 12 pills or more.

After that much aspirin, someone could easily develop heartburn or a bad stomachache. If she were to reach for the **Pepto-Bismol** to put out the fire and if the full dose of familiar pink liquid is taken, it would be roughly equivalent to eight additional aspirin tablets. That's because **Pepto-Bismol** contains bismuth subsalicylate—an aspirinlike ingredient. Added to the aspirin already swallowed, this is comparable to about 20 pills, or a total dose of 6,500 mg. That is a level capable of causing signs of aspirin overdose, which can include headache as one symptom. A headache could lead someone to take more aspirin, which in turn could lead to more stomach upset, which could lead to more **Pepto**, which could lead to ... We think you get the picture.

❑   ❑   ❑   ❑

Q. How much aspirin is too much?

A. "Too much" is a relative concept. For a child, an adult dose is too much because it could produce serious side effects. For someone with an average headache or muscle sprain, too much aspirin is anything over two regular-strength tablets: Anything more than 650 mg would be unnecessary. For someone with garden variety osteoarthritis, too much might be anything over nine or ten pills per day. People with rheumatoid arthritis, however, may need to take 12 to 18 pills daily.

Some people are especially sensitive to aspirin. For this group, even a tiny dose may be too much. Those with aspirin allergy can develop breathing problems or break out in a rash with baby aspirin. People with asthma are also more vulnerable to aspirin and can experience a bout of wheezing minutes or hours after a small dose of aspirin.

There are also some people who are susceptible to bleeding from aspirin. Virtually everyone will experience microscopic bleeding in the stomach after an oral dose. Most of us won't feel a thing or experience any adverse consequences from this minute blood loss. (Iron deficiency anemia is one possibility, though.) Others appear far more sensitive. They can develop bleeding ulcers.

More controversial is the issue of stroke. Although aspirin can prevent strokes caused by blood clots (thrombotic strokes), it may slightly increase the risk of bleeding (hemorrhagic) strokes. Some people may be more susceptible to bleeding from aspirin than others. Researchers have identified a subgroup of individuals they call hyper responders, or HRs for short.[1] These individuals are perfectly healthy, but react to even small doses of aspirin with prolonged bleeding times.

Q. What are the signs and symptoms you might experience if you were taking too much aspirin?

A. One of the first signs of taking too much aspirin is ringing in the ears and dizziness. Other symptoms include mental confusion, hearing problems, nausea, vomiting, and diarrhea. Paradoxically, some people may experience a headache from aspirin overdose. Sweating, fast breathing, flushing, thirst, and rapid pulse are other tip-offs someone is getting into danger. Such symptoms require emergency treatment.

Q. How much aspirin do you need to take to get these effects?

A. These symptoms can occur in adults at aspirin doses of 5,000 to 8,000 mg (15 to 25 pills). Children (and some older people) can experience these problems at much lower doses because they are far more sensitive to aspirin.

Q. Can you do yourself serious harm if you take excessive aspirin doses?

A. You certainly can. In addition to the symptoms above, other serious symptoms of aspirin overdose include disorientation, thirst, sluggishness, irritability, hyperactivity, fever, depression, hallucinations, hemorrhage, seizures, breathing problems, and coma.

Q. So you could even die of an aspirin overdose?

A. It's certainly possible. In adults, the lethal dose of aspirin can be as low as 10,000 mg (30 pills) or as high as 30,000 mg (90 pills). Children can die at much lower levels. Depending on weight and age, the lethal amount can be as little as a dozen pills or less.

❑   ❑   ❑   ❑

References

1. Fiore, Louis D., et al. "The Bleeding Time Response to Aspirin." *Am. J. Clin. Pathol.* 1990; 94:292–296.

CHAPTER 16

ASPIRIN FOR CHILDREN, OLDER PEOPLE, AND ANIMALS

Children, older people, and pets cannot safely take the same doses of aspirin that healthy people in their twenties, thirties, and forties can. For kids with the flu or chicken pox, aspirin poses special danger—Reye's syndrome. But even when that is not a threat, children require doses of aspirin that are tailored to their age and weight. If they are dehydrated or feverish, even standard doses may become toxic. One prominent sign of excess aspirin is fever, which may lead parents to give more aspirin, which in turn can cause more dehydration and fever. Overdose can lead to life-threatening changes in blood pH (metabolic acidosis), blood sugar, and electrolytes (depletion of potassium and sodium).

Infants should never receive aspirin unless a pediatrician specifically prescribes it. This prohibition includes nursing babies. Aspirin and other salicylates can get into breast milk. Anyone who is breast feeding should avoid aspirin unless told by a physician that occasional small doses are appropriate.

Older people are vulnerable to aspirin toxicity. They may bruise more easily, experience ringing in the ears, or develop a bleeding ulcer. Sometimes the elderly can develop salicylate "intoxication" without realizing it. They can experience a buildup of fluid in the lungs, mental confusion, headache, dizziness, hearing loss, impaired vision, ringing in the ears, and fatigue. Such symptoms could all be dismissed as consequences of aging. If ignored, they could lead to further deterioration. Additional complications include rapid breathing, sweating, nausea, vomiting, diarrhea, unusual thirst, and convulsions. Ultimately, aspirin poisoning can cause severe breathing problems, coma, cardiovascular collapse, and death.

As people age, they often end up taking a variety of other medicines. Drug interactions with aspirin can make older people especially susceptible to adverse reactions. For example, the arthritis medicine **Rheumatrex** (methotrexate) can become extremely hazardous in combination with aspirin. See Appendix III at the end of this book for other dangerous drug interactions with aspirin.

People aren't the only ones who must be careful about toxicity. Pets are incredibly sensitive to aspirin. As little as one regular-strength aspirin tablet could kill a cat. Dogs can hemorrhage from their digestive tracts after an adult dose of aspirin. Never give any human medicine to an animal without first checking with a veterinarian.

❑   ❑   ❑   ❑

Q. What is Reye's syndrome, and is it true I should not give my kids aspirin because of it?

A. Reye's syndrome is a rare but very serious condition. Symptoms include irritability, personality changes, vomiting, lethargy, delirium, and ultimately coma. Children and teenagers MUST avoid aspirin if they have the flu or chicken pox. The relationship between Reye's syndrome and aspirin has been extremely controversial. Initially, many health experts refused to believe there could be a connection. One neurologist insisted to us that cases of

Reye's syndrome after aspirin were as likely as poop under a hobby horse.

Even after an association was suspected, a warning label was delayed for five years while more data was collected. Although the Centers for Disease Control (CDC) urged the Food and Drug Administration to require a warning on the label in 1981, it wasn't until 1986 that the agency actually acted to issue such regulations.

One of this country's leading epidemiologists, Devra Lee Davis, and her colleague Patricia Buffler suggest that "during the 5 years that labeling was under consideration, about 1,700 deaths due to Reye's syndrome occurred, whereas only about 230 would have been expected if labeling had been in place during this same period. These 1,470 excess deaths are especially tragic, because they were, typically, healthy children who never recovered from viral infection or chicken pox."[1]

Q. What special guidelines should I follow when giving aspirin to my three kids? They are 12, 9, and 5.

A. The standard recommendation for dosing children with aspirin is based on age. Kids who are 2 through 3 are supposed to get 160 mg (two baby aspirins). Children 4 through 5 get 240 mg (three baby aspirins). For 6- through 8-year-olds, the recommendation is 320 mg (four baby aspirins). For 9- through 10-year-olds, 400 mg (five chewable baby aspirins). Eleven-year-olds get 486 mg (six tablets), and those 12 and over get 648 mg, or eight baby aspirin pills.

We have never liked these dosing plans because they do not take into account a child's size or weight. Several pediatricians polled their colleagues and discovered that dosing regimens can vary all over the place. They came up with a simple formula that relies on weight.[2] We have calculated that their recommendation equals one baby aspirin tablet (81 mg) for every 12 pounds of body weight.

Here's how to calculate a precise dose. If a child weighs

36 pounds, just divide by 12 and you get three baby aspirins. If the child weighs 54 pounds, the division yields four
and a half pills. A 72-pound child would get six 81-mg
chewable tablets. To be safe, always check with a pediatrician for the precise dose.

Children should never get more than five doses of aspirin
in any given 24-hour period and should not get aspirin for
more than five days unless under a doctor's care. Of course,
no child should ever get aspirin if their symptoms seem due
to chicken pox or the flu.

**Q. My mother just turned 80. She has taken large doses
of aspirin for the past ten years for her arthritis. Her doctor recently lowered the dose of some of her other drugs,
explaining that her metabolism had slowed down. Would
it be a good idea to lower her dose of aspirin for the same
reason?**

A. This might be an excellent plan. But we suggest that it
is not a trial and error process. Please have her physician
evaluate her dosing plan to match the correct amount for
her age and weight.

**Q. My father was hospitalized with a bleeding ulcer last
year. The doctor blamed it on the aspirin my father has
taken for years for his rheumatism. Dad wants to take
aspirin again because it's a lot less expensive than the
medicine his doctor prescribed. Is this safe, given his
past history?**

A. Discourage your dad from taking aspirin on his own.
Unless his doctor specifically recommends it, aspirin could
be too dangerous for him. If he complains about expense,
have him add the cost of hospitalization to the price tag he
pays at the drug store. By the way, most of the prescription
arthritis medicines can also cause ulcers, so make sure your
father's doctor is monitoring him closely.

Q. What daily dose of aspirin should we give our 17-year-old, 25-pound terrier for arthritis? For toothache? How about our 3-year-old, 6-pound tabby cat?

A. Doses for animals are significantly different than for people. Dogs metabolize aspirin more slowly than humans, and so only need a dose of aspirin every 8 to 18 hours. They are also more vulnerable to digestive tract upset and ulceration. Dogs can die from a perforated bleeding ulcer. Cats are even more sensitive. They can tolerate aspirin only every three days.

As dogs get older their kidneys and livers begin to work less efficiently—just like humans. Your dog should be able to stand between 5 and 10 mg of aspirin per kilogram of weight. Since your dog weighs 11.4 kg, that means one baby aspirin (81 mg) twice a day. Because aspirin is so irritating to the stomach it should be given only at meal time. Cats should get no more than one baby aspirin every three days. Check with your vet for exact dosing instructions to be on the safe side.

Q. My neighbor gives aspirin to her golden retriever, who suffers from arthritis in her hips. Is this a good idea? What about Advil or Tylenol? Can you safely give them to animals?

A. Arthritic dogs often get small doses of aspirin from a vet. They should only take two doses a day, though, since they are more susceptible to stomach problems than people. The dosage range is 5 to 10 mg/kg of aspirin a day. Big dogs should get buffered aspirin, like **Ascriptin**, to minimize the stomach irritation.

Do not give ibuprofen like **Advil** or **Motrin IB** as it can be far too irritating to the intestinal tract. Two tablets could represent a serious overdose. Cats are even more vulnerable to ibuprofen and acetaminophen (**Tylenol**, etc.). As little as one tablet of acetaminophen could kill a cat within a few days. Always check with your vet to protect your animal's health.

❑   ❑   ❑   ❑

References

1. Davis, Devra Lee and Buffler, Patricia. "Reduction of Deaths After Drug Labelling for Risk of Reye's Syndrome." *Lancet* 1992; 340:1042.
2. Done, Alan K., et al. "Aspirin Dosage for Infants." *J. of Ped.* 1979; 95:617–624.

CHAPTER 17

GUIDELINES FOR BUYING, STORING, AND TAKING ASPIRIN

Because people take aspirin for granted, they tend to buy huge quantities (sometimes 500 pills to the bottle) and then leave them in the darndest places. We have seen open aspirin bottles in steamy locker rooms, in glove compartments, in old first-aid kits, and one time we found some aspirin in a fishing tackle box. The problem is that aspirin can deteriorate, especially if it is in a childproof bottle that has a cap that is not air tight. Humidity can speed the process of chemical breakdown. The best way to tell if your aspirin is beginning to go bad is to smell it. An acid vinegarlike odor suggests that acetylsalicylic acid is beginning to turn to acetic acid (vinegar). That might be a good sign to reinvest in a new bottle.

❑   ❑   ❑   ❑

Q. I am a 67-year-old woman, but I weigh only 88 pounds. I take aspirin occasionally for headaches or sprains. Should I take a regular adult dose of aspirin, or do I need a smaller dose?

A. The standard adult dose for these conditions is 325 to 650 mg (one or two pills). Adults of less than average weight should probably start with one tablet every four hours. If that is ineffective, two regular-strength tablets are certainly appropriate.

Q. I am 6 feet 6 inches tall and have always been heavyset. But lately I have put on so much lard that I now look like your proverbial fat guy. I won't tell you my weight, but suffice it to say that I require a special scale. I frequently take aspirin for a painful bad back. If guidelines for drug use were based on body weight, I would probably need a whole bottle of aspirin at a time. What do you think? Should I take a larger than average dose?

A. Even people who are on the heavy side can benefit from one to two regular-strength aspirin tablets. If that dose doesn't work, you might increase your dose to three pills (975 mg) every six hours for a short period of time. Check with your physician to be safe.

A number of preparations come in higher doses: **Ascriptin Extra Strength** (500 mg), **Alka-Seltzer Extra Strength** (500 mg), **Maximum Bayer** (500 mg), **Maximum Strength Ecotrin** (500 mg), **Extra Strength Bufferin** (500 mg), **A.S.A. Enseals** (650 mg), **Arthritis Strength BC Powder** (742 mg), and prescription-strength **Easprin** (975 mg).

Q. Should aspirin be stored in any special place? Kept away from light? Does it last longer if kept in the refrigerator or freezer?

A. Keep aspirin away from heat, light, and moisture. Always remove the cotton stuffing, which can absorb moisture and speed deterioration. The optimum temperature range for storage is between 59 degrees and 86 degrees Fahrenheit. Keep aspirin in an airtight container. Some childproof caps are not airtight and therefore may speed breakdown. Do not store in a refrigerator.

Smell aspirin to determine if it has begun to deteriorate.
An acid or vinegary smell indicates that aspirin has begun
to break down to acetic acid, or vinegar. That doesn't make
it dangerous, just less potent. However, most standard reference books recommend against using aspirin if it has a
strong odor of vinegar.

**Q. Why is it that almost all aspirin comes packaged in
325-mg (5 grain) tablets? What other sizes are available?
Where do you get them?**

A. The dose of aspirin we use today is based on grains, an
old apothecary measure popular when aspirin first came on
the market—nearly 100 years ago. In those days a standard
dose of aspirin was 10 grains. One grain equals 64.8 mg
(milligrams), so a standard dose was ten times that, or 648
mg.

Each regular-strength aspirin tablet should in reality be
half that amount or 324 mg—a rather odd amount to say
the least. Most makers of aspirin round off to 325 mg for
a regular-strength tablet, which equals 5 grains.

Although the standard aspirin pill is 5 grains, that hasn't
inhibited drug makers from coming up with all sorts of
innovative dosage forms. The lowest dose comes in suppository form (60 mg). Aspirin suppositories also come in
120-mg, 125-mg, 130-mg, 195-mg, 200- mg, 300-mg, 325-
mg, 600-mg, 650-mg, and 1,200-mg forms.

The lowest oral dose is "baby" aspirin, which weighs
in at the oddball amount of 81 mg. (This is one quarter of
a standard adult tablet.) By the way, you can get **St. Joseph
Low Dose Adult Aspirin** in 81 mg, chewable tablets. This
is an expensive way to get low-dose aspirin, though. A
small bottle (36 pills) can cost up to $2.00 for a brand name
product, which is outrageous when you can buy 300 regular-strength tablets for less than $2.00.

There are all sorts of other aspirin doses on the market:
130 mg in **Dasin**, 228 mg in **Aspergum**, 240.5 mg in **Dol-
cin**, 260 mg in **Panodynes Analgesic**, 325 mg in **Bayer**,

357 mg in **Emagrin**, 400 mg in **Anacin**, 420.6 mg in **Anodynos**, 421 mg in **Cope**, 454 mg in **Midol Caplets Original Formula**, 500 mg in **Arthritis Pain Formula**, 520 mg in **Goody's Headache Powder**, 650 mg in **8-Hour Bayer Caplets** and **Measurin Timed-Release**, 742 mg in **BC Arthritis Strength Powder**, and 850 mg in **Stanback Max Powder**. Prescription-strength aspirin comes in **Easprin** (975 mg enteric-coated tablets).

Q. I have great trouble swallowing my three aspirins every four hours. My throat was not designed for swallowing pills. I cough. I retch. Isn't there an easier way?

A. It is important that you do everything possible to avoid having aspirin get stuck in your throat. Leaving aspirin in contact with the lining of the esophagus can result in serious irritation. That is why it is imperative that aspirin always be swallowed with a full glass of water while standing. Ideally, remain upright for 15 to 30 minutes after swallowing aspirin to make sure it does not get stuck.

If swallowing three pills is a problem, there are several options. You could ask your doctor for a prescription for **Easprin**—coated aspirin that comes with 975 mg per tablet. That is the equivalent of three pills in one. There is also liquid aspirin in the form of **Alka-Seltzer**. The plopping and fizzing will dissolve the tablet and it will go down the hatch smooth as silk. Unfortunately, that is an expensive way to get aspirin on a regular basis. It will also expose you to a high dose of sodium. A cheap alternative to this would be to drop two aspirin tablets in a glass of carbonated mineral water and wait for them to dissolve.

Other liquid-based approaches include the aspirin powders. You can buy **BC Powder** (650 mg per packet), **Goody's Headache Powder** (520 mg), and **Stanback Powder** (650 mg and 850 mg). Unfortunately, all three powder products also contain additional analgesics like salicylamide or acetaminophen and also caffeine. Regular use of combination pain relievers may pose a hazard of kidney damage.

One other possibility is a product called **Arthropan** (choline salicylate). It comes in a liquid (870 mg per teaspoon), so it should be easy to swallow. The active ingredient, choline salicylate, is similar to aspirin but is less likely to irritate the digestive tract than aspirin. Although **Arthropan** is good for inflammation and therefore a reasonable option for people with arthritis, it may be a little less effective than aspirin at relieving pain.

Finally, don't rule out aspirin suppositories. They come in a wide variety of doses and bypass the stomach entirely. We are a little squeamish about this method of taking medicines in this country, but Europeans find this a very acceptable dosage form. And you certainly won't have to worry about the aspirin getting stuck in your throat.

Q. Can you recommend a good mail-order source of unusual forms of aspirin—liquid, small doses, etc.

A. It can be hard to find low-dose aspirin at a reasonable price. One mail-order firm that is highly reputable is Bronson Pharmaceuticals (La Canada, California 91011). It charges less that $7.00 for 180 pills (81 mg). AARP (American Association of Retired Persons) has a mail-order pharmacy program that also sells inexpensive low dose (one fourth tablet) aspirin in bottles of 1,000 pills. For order information call (800) 456-4636.

Q. Is it better to take aspirin with water or milk? How about carbonated beverages—are they okay too? What are the pros and cons of mashing up the tablet and taking it with applesauce? If you take aspirin via this route, would you follow up with a liquid "chaser," too?

A. Aspirin can be taken with water, milk, or juice. The less acidic the beverage, though, the more likely aspirin will be rapidly absorbed. Chase that aspirin with a full eight-ounce glass of liquid to help dissolve the pill and reduce stomach irritation.

Mashing an aspirin tablet with mortar and pestle will

reduce the likelihood that a little chunk of the tablet will sit in a pocket of your stomach and cause damage. Food does slow absorption a little, but the benefits seem to outweigh any delay. If you mix the aspirin powder with applesauce or pudding, we do recommend that you still drink a glass of water to enhance absorption and reduce irritation.

Q. Is it better to take aspirin during the day or at bedtime?

A. This is a very sophisticated question because there is some research to suggest that the time of day can affect the blood levels of certain drugs. Pain itself can vary over the course of the day. For example, after surgery some patients may need more morphine in the morning than in the afternoon. Some arthritis medicines appear more effective when taken at certain times of the day. We have not been able to find any documentation about aspirin, however, and so you would be better off checking with your physician to arrange a dosing schedule that best suits your situation.

Q. What are the most important things to keep in mind when I'm at the drugstore, standing in front of that well-stocked counter that holds the various types of aspirin and similar drugs?

A. Aspirin is aspirin is acetylsalicylic acid. You can pay more for brand name products, but house brand aspirin will be just as effective. It contains exactly the same active ingredient. You may prefer the texture, coating or reassurance of a particular brand-name product. It's your choice.

Q. I sometimes put my aspirin in orange or grapefruit juice and let it dissolve before taking it. But I worry that the acid in these juices might upset my stomach—or might have some effect on the aspirin working in my system.

A. We can think of no reason why dissolving your aspirin ahead of time would diminish its effectiveness or increase your risk of stomach irritation. If anything, the dissolved aspirin will be easier on your tummy.

You must be very patient to wait for aspirin to dissolve in juice, though. When we put aspirin in OJ it just sits at the bottom of the glass for a long time. If you are swallowing pills, we discourage acidic beverages like orange juice, as they may slow absorption. Milk or water would be a better way to go. Always drink a full 8 ounces to maximize absorption and diminish stomach upset.

Q. Does aspirin spoil or expire after a certain period? How long does this usually take? Can hot weather speed this process? How can I tell when a bottle of aspirin is no good?

A. Like all drugs, aspirin can deteriorate over time. One of the breakdown products is acetic acid (vinegar) so if you detect a vinegarlike odor when you open the bottle, your aspirin has begun to go bad. This doesn't mean it will be harmful, just that it has begun to lose potency.

Storing aspirin in a cool (59 to 86 degrees Fahrenheit), dry place is the best way to keep it effective. Take the cotton stuffing material out. It is only there to keep the pills from bouncing around during shipping. Cotton can harbor moisture, which is not good for any medicine.

❏   ❏   ❏   ❏

IV

BRANDS, TYPES, AND FORMS OF ASPIRIN

CHAPTER 18

ASPIRIN IN COMBINATION: ANACIN, EXCEDRIN, VANQUISH, ETC.

Sometimes we wish drug companies would just leave well enough alone. Aspirin is a great drug—all by itself. Why add other pain relievers or extra ingredients to confuse the issue? But marketing being what it is, we're not surprised that Madison Avenue would want to try to make a better mousetrap. The pain reliever market is a multi-billion dollar industry and competition is fierce. Companies that have a successful and highly recognized brand name try to capitalize on their good reputation by expanding into a number of different niches.

Take the popular pain reliever **Alka-Seltzer**. Once upon a time it contained nothing more than aspirin, the antacid sodium bicarbonate (baking soda), and citric acid to help it fizz. Nowadays, there are at least eight different **Alka-Seltzer** formulations to treat a wide variety of ills. There is **Alka-Seltzer Extra Strength, Alka-Seltzer Plus Cold Medicine, Alka-Seltzer Plus Night-Time Cold Medicine,** and even **Alka-Seltzer Advanced Formula Antacid & Non-Aspirin Pain Reliever.**

In addition to special nighttime formulations with the sedating antihistamine diphenhydramine, many manufacturers have developed products for sinus headaches, allergies, backaches, and colds and flu. The hot toddy approach has been particularly successful. Companies market packets of powdered pain relievers, antihistamines, decongestants, and cough suppressants. There is also flavoring, so that when the mix is dumped into a mug and dissolved in hot water, it is reminiscent of Grandma's tea with honey and lemon or that French cold favorite, the hot toddy. Such products often cost double or triple the price of conventional cold remedies.

By adding so many ingredients to a perfectly good pain reliever, the companies come up with a marketer's dream come true. But health experts question the value of this shotgun approach. The more drugs you put into a formulation, the more likely it is that there will be undesirable side effects. Concerns have been raised that taking multiple analgesics may increase the risk of kidney damage. We tend to recommend pure aspirin for pain or inflammation. It is hard to improve upon plain-Jane aspirin's success.

❑   ❑   ❑   ❑

Q. I have heard that aspirin plus caffeine is better for some people's headaches. Is this true? It is hard to imagine how this would be so, as I always found that coffee-drinking caused headaches. Which aspirin products contain caffeine?

A. The value of caffeine in boosting the pain-relieving effect of aspirin has been highly controversial. For years scientists debated whether adding caffeine to aspirin or other pain relievers was anything more than a marketing gimmick. For example, **Anacin** (400 mg of aspirin and 32 mg of caffeine per pill) has touted its special formulation for years.

But research now seems to suggest that caffeine does indeed provide additional benefit. One double-blind study sponsored by the manufacturer of **Anacin** demonstrated that caffeine and aspirin was superior to plain acetaminophen in relieving tension headaches.[1] Several other reports suggest that caffeine (about the amount found in a weak cup of coffee) can enhance the relief of pain due to oral surgery, episiotomies, and sore throats.[2,3,4]

The marketplace has also spoken loudly on this issue. When several manufacturers removed caffeine from their pain relievers, market share plummeted. People may not read labels to see what the product contains, but they seem to realize when caffeine is removed from their favored analgesic.

Does this mean you have to spend lots on brand name products like **Anacin, BC Tablets** or **Powders, Excedrin Extra-Strength, Midol,** and **Vanquish**? Clearly not. You could just buy generic aspirin and swallow it with a soft drink that contains caffeine (**Coke, Dr. Pepper, Pepsi, Mello Yello, Mountain Dew,** etc.). You could also drink a cup of coffee or tea in conjunction with your aspirin. There are even some generic aspirin and caffeine combinations available, so ask your pharmacist.

There is a word of caution about caffeine, however. Repeated use of such products may set up a vicious cycle that actually perpetuates headaches because of caffeine withdrawal. As little as two or three cups of coffee (235 mg of caffeine) on a regular basis can lead to symptoms of headache, fatigue, and anxiety upon sudden discontinuation.[5]

Chronic use of prescription headache medicines that contain caffeine (such as **Fiorinal**) may actually contribute to the very headaches they are supposed to alleviate.[6] As the effect of the caffeine wears off, the unsuspecting headache victim may be led to repeated dosing. Whether the product is prescription or over-the-counter, we advise caution when using a combination pain reliever containing caffeine.

Q. I used to count on Empirin Compound to take away my headaches better than any other pain reliever on the market. I haven't seen it in years, and plain Empirin isn't the same. Is there anything else that contains the same ingredients as Empirin Compound?

A. Empirin Compound contained aspirin, phenacetin, and caffeine, the same ingredients that were so popular in **APC** tablets. Such products are no longer available because the FDA required the removal of phenacetin. Regular use was linked to a higher risk of kidney disease and kidney failure. Because the kidney is so crucial in eliminating drugs from the body, it seems to be especially vulnerable to chronic exposure.

Q. Since aspirin has similar effects to acetaminophen and ibuprofen, wouldn't you be better off taking all three at once?

A. There is no data to suggest that putting two or three of these pain relievers together will add to total analgesic effect. You might think that adding high-test gasoline to an old clunker will make it run better. Not true. There is only so much you can ask of a car or a pain reliever. Health experts suspect that combining aspirin with other pain relievers may increase the risk of kidney damage, especially if they are used on a regular basis. Without good epidemiological data on the question, the FDA has not taken a stand, but we like to err on the side of caution. Until we know more about this crucial safety issue, why not stick to single-ingredient pain relievers?

Q. I had my wisdom teeth removed three years ago, and was given a prescription for Empirin with Codeine No. 3. It worked extremely well, but fortunately I didn't need to use all the pills. I have saved them for times when I need strong pain relief, like when my back goes out. How long can I keep these pills?

A. Empirin No. 3 contains 325 mg aspirin and 30 mg of codeine in each tablet. This is the one situation in which a combination pain reliever makes sense to us. For really bad pain, adding codeine to either aspirin or acetaminophen produces a very effective analgesic. It is available only by prescription because codeine is a narcotic and can be addicting, when it is taken for an extended period.

We don't encourage anyone to hoard pain pills, though. Drugs deteriorate over time, and we have no way of knowing how long your **Empirin** will stay good. Do ask the pharmacist to put an expiration date on every prescription you have filled in the future. This is especially important for pain medicine you won't be finishing immediately.

Q. How come my wife gets such dramatic results with BC Powder but experiences very little positive effect from any other aspirin-containing product?

A. BC Powder contains 650 mg aspirin, 195 mg salicylamide, and 32 mg caffeine. There are no other pain relievers we know of with that precise formulation. Although the experts say salicylamide is probably ineffective in doses below 300 mg, there is inadequate data on combination therapy for headache treatment. Salicylamide is not supposed to be very good for inflammation, so it is probably a poor choice if you have arthritis. It is also inferior to aspirin when it comes to treating a fever.

Powdered aspirin probably goes to work a little faster than aspirin in tablet form. We also know that caffeine can boost the benefits of aspirin, although the 32 mg in **BC** is a very low dose—about equal to a cup of tea. One way to test the hypothesis that the salicylamide is helping would be to try aspirin and caffeine with and without salicylamide. You can buy pure salicylamide in **DeWitt Pills** (108.2 mg). Two **DeWitt Pills** taken with regular aspirin and a weak cup of coffee would approximate **BC Powder**. We would caution against long-term use of this combination without medical supervision until safety questions about the kidneys are resolved.

❑   ❑   ❑   ❑

References

1. Schactel, B.P., et al. "Headache Pain Model for Assessing and Comparing the Efficacy of Over-the-Counter Analgesic Agents." *Clin. Pharmacol. Ther.* 1991; 50:322–329.

2. Schactel, B.P., et al. "Caffeine As an Analgesic Adjuvant. A Double-Blind Study Comparing Aspirin with Caffeine to Aspirin and Placebo in Patients with Sore Throat." *Arch. Intern. Med.* 1991; 151:733–737.

3. Laska, E.M., et al. *Clin. Pharmacol. Ther.* 1983; 33:498.

4. Forbes, J.A., et al. "Evaluation of Aspirin, Caffeine, and Their Combination in Postoperative Oral Surgery Pain." *Pharmacotherapy* 1990; 10:387–393.

5. Silverman, Kenneth, et al. "Withdrawal Syndrome After the Double-Blind Cessation of Caffeine Consumption." *N. Engl. J. Med.* 1992; 327:1109–1114.

6. Sands, G.H. "A Protocol for Butalbital, Aspirin and Caffeine (BAC) Detoxification in Headache Patients." *Headache* 1990; 30:491–496.

CHAPTER 19

BRANDED VS. GENERIC, MINI-TABS, BUFFERED, AND COATED ASPIRIN

You can spend over $6.00 for a brand name pain reliever with fewer than 100 pills, or you can pay less than $2.00 for 300 aspirin tablets. Let your pocketbook be your guide. Some folks tell us that only brand name products work for them. We recognize that psychology plays an important role in pain relief. British researchers actually proved this in a clever experiment. They created a placebo pill that looked exactly like a familiar and popular brand-name aspirin product. They compared the brand-name product and its look-alike placebo to a plain aspirin tablet and a plain-appearing placebo. They were astonished that the plain placebo pill relieved headaches in 40 percent of the people studied. The fancy placebo did substantially better, even though it contained absolutely no active ingredient. They concluded that up to one third of the benefit people experience from a brand-name pain medicine can be attributed to its appearance and the psychological expectations people have.[1]

We can only say that aspirin is acetylsalicylic acid is aspirin. You pays your money and takes your chances.

Tinkerbell knew the secret that if you believe strongly enough, you can make wonderful things happen.

❑   ❑   ❑   ❑

Q. Is Bayer aspirin really better than the cheap drugstore variety?

A. Chemically they are identical. How they work in your body will depend to a degree on your expectations. There is some benefit, like the placebo effect, that will occur if you are convinced **Bayer** is better, but pharmacologically, house brand aspirin is the same.

Q. I know that you have written that the brand of aspirin makes no difference once it gets into your body. Maybe not, but I find that some brands are easier to swallow, e.g., Bayer, which seems to have a smooth coating over the pill. Cheaper aspirin is grainy and leaves a bad taste in your mouth. I can afford it, so I'm buying Bayer.

A. Great! Always use what works best for you.

Q. Is generic coated aspirin just as effective as Ecotrin and the other more expensive brands?

A. Theoretically, generic enteric-coated aspirin should work as well as any of the brand name coated aspirins. We know of no studies in which researchers have compared these two types of products. Some people insist, however, that only **Ecotrin** works for them. You will have to be your own judge.

Q. Is enteric-coated aspirin just as potent, milligram for milligram, as regular aspirin, or do you need to take more?

A. Enteric aspirin is merely a core of acetylsalicylic acid surrounded by a special coating that is pH sensitive. It is not supposed to dissolve at the low pH (high acid level) that is the normal environment of the stomach. When the coated aspirin passes into the small intestine, the coating dissolves at the higher pH of the new, more neutral or alkaline environment.

Coated aspirin comes in a variety of doses from 325 mg (regular strength) to 500 mg (maximum or "therapy" strength) up to prescription strength (975 mg). It should be just as potent milligram for milligram as any other aspirin formulation, though some people may find it takes longer to experience headache relief because of the time needed to pass into the small intestine.

Q. I want to know about the other contents of these enteric-coated aspirin pills. What are the substances in the coating (dyes, chemicals, etc.) and how do they affect my body?

A. Ecotrin, the leading brand of enteric-coated aspirin, contains 325 mg of aspirin as its active ingredient. The inactive ingredients in the pill and coating include dyes (D&C Yellow No. 10 and FD&C Yellow No. 6) as well as cellulose, cellulose acetate phthalate, diethyl phthalate, silicon dioxide, sodium starch glycolate, starch, stearic acid, titanium dioxide, and traces of other inactive ingredients.

Therapy Bayer Enteric Aspirin is another brand name enteric-coated aspirin. It contains D&C Yellow No. 10, FD&C Yellow No. 6, hydroxypropyl methylcellulose, methacrylic acid, copolymer, starch, titanium dioxide, triacetin, polysorbate 80, and sodium lauryl sulfate.

We don't have good studies to help us decide how such "inactive" ingredients may affect your body. Some people are more susceptible to dyes, especially tartrazine (FD&C Yellow No. 5) than others. But trying to unravel reactions to inactive ingredients can be tricky. Check the inactive ingredients list on the label to find out exactly what's in the brand you take.

Q. Can you tell me where to find a coated aspirin tablet in a 150- to 175-mg dose? My doctor told me to take this

dose daily and my stomach can't tolerate uncoated aspirin.

A. Enteric-coated, low-dose aspirin products include **Halfprin** (165 mg of aspirin), **Adult Analgesic 1/2 Halfprin** (81 mg), and **Bayer Enteric Safety Coated** (81 mg).

Q. Is it okay for people who don't have ulcers to take coated aspirin? Is this advisable?

A. Aspirin can be irritating to the stomach even for people without ulcers. Enteric-coated aspirin is no absolute guarantee of safety, but it does cut down on direct irritation to the stomach lining. It accomplishes this by dissolving in the small intestine, where the environment is less acidic.

The manufacturers of brand name enteric-coated aspirin maintain that their products perform comparably to regular aspirin. But concerns have been raised that "aspirin absorption from enteric-coated tablets may be highly erratic. Tablets sometimes dissolve prematurely in the stomach and sometimes they do not dissolve at all."[2] You will have to be the judge as to whether enteric-coated aspirin is worth the extra price.

Q. I don't understand how buffered aspirin can work. Doesn't the buffer work to change it to alkaline, while aspirin is an acid? Very confusing to me. Please explain.

A. The buffering compounds that are often added to aspirin include aluminum and magnesium hydroxide, calcium carbonate, and sodium bicarbonate. The alkaline environment created by these buffers helps aspirin dissolve faster and therefore decreases the length of time irritating aspirin particles remain in contact with sensitive stomach tissue.

Q. Doesn't coated aspirin take a lot longer to act than the uncoated kind?

A. Since coated aspirin is theoretically designed to dissolve in the small intestine rather than in the stomach, there is likely to be some delay in absorption. Whether it is clinically significant for arthritis is doubtful. For quick headache relief, though, you might be better off with a soluble product such as **Alka-Seltzer**, a headache powder, or just regular aspirin that you swallow with an 8-ounce glass of water.

Q. Coated aspirin may help protect the stomach, but isn't it a lot harder on the small intestine? You can get an ulcer there too, you know.

A. Coated aspirin is designed to dissolve in the more alkaline environment of the small intestine, rather than the low-pH acid environment of the stomach. While this reduces stomach upset and ulceration, it does not eliminate problems entirely. Some people still develop symptoms and ulcers. There is an additional possibility that coated aspirin could produce irritation and ulcerations in the small intestine. Warnings to this effect are not included in standard medical references, but we share your concern. People rarely complain of pain or discomfort from lesions in the small intestine, but a perforated ulcer in that region of the digestive tract could be quite serious.

Q. Does Aspergum do any good for a sore throat, or would you be better off taking plain aspirin?

A. Although people assume that **Aspergum** is good for sore throats, there is no reason to believe that this formulation would be any better than plain aspirin. **Aspergum** probably exerts its pain-relieving effect through the blood stream, rather than direct contact with the throat. Any effect aspirin has on the throat as it passes into the stomach is temporary at best. In fact, the best recommendation is to drink a glass of water after chewing **Aspergum** in order to facilitate absorption from the stomach. This would obviously wash any residue right into the stomach.

Each piece of **Aspergum** contains 227 mg of aspirin. Children must not think of this as candy or chewing gum that they can take on their own. Only one "tablet" should be administered to children 3 to 6 years of age. More than that could result in toxicity.

Adults who have trouble swallowing pills might want to consider **Aspergum** as an alternative. Two pieces of gum would almost equal the amount of aspirin in products like **Maximum Strength Anacin** or **Extra Strength Ascriptin** (500 mg). For arthritis pain or a muscle strain one could conceivably chew three or four pieces and get a dose that would provide relief. We know of no studies confirming this, however.

Q. I take one coated aspirin per day at my cardiologist's recommendation. I already have an ulcer and these coated pills don't seem to bother it. But I worry: Are they as effective as regular aspirin?

A. For the purposes of thinning the blood and preventing blood clots, one enteric-coated aspirin daily should be more than adequate. Although questions have been raised about absorption, most people find coated aspirin as effective as regular aspirin.

Of greater concern is your history of stomach problems. People with ulcers who continue to take enteric-coated aspirin have a hard time healing their lesions, even when they take ulcer medicines like cimetidine or antacids.[3]

Q. I take 10 grams of a generic coated aspirin three times per day for rheumatoid spondylitis. I have been doing this for many years with no ill effects so far. But I worry. Does coated aspirin really protect the stomach over long periods of time as opposed to regular aspirin?

A. People who rely on enteric-coated aspirin seem to experience a little less indigestion, heartburn, and other symptoms of stomach upset than those taking regular aspirin. There may even be a little less injury to the stomach lining.[4] There is no guarantee, however, that coated aspirin really protects the stomach over long periods of time. People who rely on enteric-coated aspirin for chronic conditions like arthritis can still develop ulcers, sometimes without early warning signs of trouble.[5] Remember, aspirin can cause stomach irritation through an indirect, systemic effect.

Q. I am taking Easprin, but it has gotten awfully expensive. Is there a generic equivalent or cheaper form?

A. Easprin is a prescription-strength high-dose (975 mg) enteric-coated aspirin. That means it packs a huge aspirin dose in a pill that is supposed to be a little less irritating to the stomach. We know of no comparable generic formulation.

Why not take over-the-counter enteric-coated aspirin in a smaller dose? You could get generic aspirin that is coated or you could buy Lilly's brand (**A.S.A. Enseals**) or Bayer's brand (**Therapy Bayer Caplets**) or SmithKline's brand (**Ecotrin**). Three of these 325-mg coated aspirin tablets would be equal to one **Easprin**. If swallowing that many pills concerns you, there are high-dose coated aspirin pills such as **Maximum Strength Ecotrin** (500 mg) and **A.S.A. Enseals** that come in 650-mg tablets.

Q. I have been told that I need to take a baby aspirin a day to help thin my blood. I also need to take a coated aspirin due to an ulcer. I am unable to find enteric-coated baby aspirin. The smallest coated aspirin I can find is 325 mg. Can you give me a source for coated baby aspirin?

A. We're not sure you should be taking aspirin at all if you have an ulcer. Double check with your physician to make sure aspirin is really appropriate. If it is, you might check the drugstore for **Bayer Enteric Safety Coated** (81 mg) or **Adult Analgesic 1/2 Halfprin** (81 mg). Both are enteric-coated at a baby aspirin dose, designed strictly for adults.

❑   ❑   ❑   ❑

References

1. Braithwaite, A., and Cooper, P. "Analgesic Effects of Branding in Treatment of Headaches." *Brit. Med. J.* 1981; 282: 1576–1578.

2. Van Tyle, W. Kent. "Internal Analgesic Products," in Feldmann, Edward G., et al.: *Handbook of Nonprescription Drugs*, 9th ed. Washington, D.C.: American Pharmaceutical Association, 1990, pp. 64–65.

3. Jaszewski, R., et al. "Persistence of Gastric Ulcers Caused by Plain Aspirin or Nonsteroidal Anti-inflammatory Agents in Patients Treated with a Combination of Cimetidine, Antacids, and Enteric-Coated Aspirin." *Dig. Dis. Sci.* 1989; 34: 1361–1364.

4. Lanza, L.F. "A Review of Gastric Ulcer and Gastroduodenal Injury in Normal Volunteers Receiving Aspirin and Other Non-Steroidal Anti-Inflammatory Drugs." *Scand. J. Gastroenterol. Suppl.* 1989; 163:24–31.

5. Jaszewski, R. "Frequency of Gastroduodenal Lesions in Asymptomatic Patients on Chronic Aspirin or Nonsteroidal Anti-inflammatory Drug Therapy." *J. Clin. Gastroenterol.* 1990; 12:10–13.

CHAPTER 20

ASPIRIN'S KISSING COUSINS

Aspirin is the most famous and popular salicylate on the market. But it is by no means the only drug in this family. Willow bark, which was the first natural salicyate discovered, contained the active ingredient salicin, also known as salicylic acid. Synthetic salicylates soon followed, including sodium salicylate and acetysalicylic acid (aspirin). All the salicylates have the ability to ease pain, lower a fever, and relieve inflammation. But aspirin seems stronger when it comes to blocking prostaglandin formation. This makes it a better anti-inflammatory agent and therefore a little more effective against arthritis. Aspirin is also the only drug in this class that irreversibly prevents platelets from clumping together. This means that only aspirin has been shown to help protect against blood clots, strokes, and heart attacks. Scientists think it is the *acetyl* part of acetylsalicylic acid that accounts for this unique action.

Just because the other salicylates can't prevent blood clots doesn't make them worthless. Many of these alternate forms of aspirin may offer benefits over regular aspirin. For example, some appear to be significantly less irritating to the stomach lining. This can be very helpful to someone who needs to take large doses for arthritis or another chronic condition. In addition, some may work better than aspirin in certain situations. They appear to be somewhat less likely to cause bleeding problems, for example. Most of the aspirinlike salicylates are available only by prescription, so you will need to discuss safety and effectiveness with a physician before considering these options.

□   □   □   □

Q. Can you list the other aspirinlike drugs—besides standard aspirin?

A. Aspirinlike drugs include:

- Choline salicylate
- Magnesium salicylate
- Salsalate
- Choline magnesium trisalicylate
- Sodium salicylate

Q. Perhaps you could describe those one at a time?

A. Gladly. Here's your list:

Choline salicylate (**Arthropan**) is available in liquid form (mint flavor) and is especially helpful for those who have trouble swallowing pills. It can be purchased without a prescription and is less likely to cause stomach upset than aspirin. Unfortunately, choline salicylate is less effective at easing pain and lowering fever than aspirin, though it will relieve inflammation for people with arthritis. To obtain an equivalent effect, you would have to swallow 435 mg of **Arthropan** for each 325 mg of aspirin. **Arthropan** does not affect platelets and therefore should not be used to guard against heart attack or stroke.

Magnesium salicylate (**Doan's Original** and **Extra Strength Doan's**) might also be a little less likely to cause stomach upset than aspirin. It may also be less effective than aspirin at relieving pain and reducing a fever, though it should help with inflammation. Despite the past advertising, **Doan's** has no special ability to relieve a backache over aspirin or other aspirinlike products. People with kidney problems must be very careful about magnesium-containing products as they can be quite toxic. In such a case **Doan's** should be taken only under a doctor's supervision, if at all. If magnesium salicylate is the best choice, the doctor may prefer to prescribe **Magan** (545 mg) or **Mobidin** (600 mg), which offer slightly more pain reliever than the OTC **Doan's**.

Salsalate (salicylsalicylic acid) is insoluble in the stomach and is only absorbed when it gets to the small intestine. In one study salsalate was equally as effective as aspirin in relieving joint pain and morning stiffness with less stomach pain and GI bleeding.[1] The downside of salsalate is that it may cause a little more dizziness and hearing problems than aspirin. It is also available only by prescription (**Amigesic, Artha-G, Disalcid, Mono-Gesic, Salflex,** and **Salsitab**). You will have to discuss this alternative with your physician. Salsalate is not supposed to affect platelets, so it may not provide protection against heart attacks or strokes the way aspirin does. That also means it is less likely to cause bleeding problems.

Choline magnesium trisalicylate (**Trilisate, Tricosal, Trisalicylate**) is available only by prescription. It has been shown to be less likely to cause stomach problems than aspirin.[2] **Trilisate** comes in either tablet or liquid formulas.

In one study of arthritis patients aspirin caused intolerable digestive tract toxicity in about 20 percent, while **Trilisate** affected only 10 percent so severely.[3] It does not change blood platelets, so **Trilisate** probably won't protect against heart attacks or strokes.

No matter which aspirinlike pain reliever is selected, caution is always called for. While many of these options can be a little easier on the tummy, none is perfectly safe. If symptoms of indigestion or heartburn develop, please see a health professional.

Q. How about salicylic acid, the "daddy" of present day aspirin? What are the pros and cons of that?

Sodium salicylate. The "granddaddy" of aspirin was actually willow bark, a natural product known for centuries to provide medicinal benefits against fevers and pain. It was the first of the salicylates, with its active ingredient, salicin, purified in 1829. In the body salicin is converted into salicylic acid.

One of the first synthetic salicylates to be used medicinally was sodium salicylate. Doctors treated rheumatic fever with this compound in 1875 and shortly thereafter employed it against gout. Acetylsalicylic acid (aspirin) was first synthesized in 1853 but not actually used by doctors until 1899.

Sodium salicylate became extremely successful. It is still available today in a generic form or as **Uracel 5**. It is a little less effective than aspirin in reducing fever and controlling pain, but people who are allergic to aspirin may be able to take sodium salicylate. This compound does not affect blood platelets, so it may not be as effective as aspirin against heart attack or stroke. The sodium content is high enough to cause problems for those people on salt-restricted diets.

Salicylamide is not officially a salicylate even though it is chemically quite similar. There has been considerable controversy about the benefits of salicylamide. According to the *Handbook of Nonprescription Drugs,* the Food and Drug Administration's expert panel did not think very highly of salicylamide's analgesic action. Even in combination with other medicines that reduce fever and relieve pain, salicylamide may not provide substantial improvement.[4]

Despite such a negative analysis, salicylamide is found combined with aspirin in a number of pain relievers, including **BC Tablets and Powder, Emagrin, Panodynes Analgesic, Presalin, Saleto, Salocol, Stanback Powder, Tri-Pain Caplets,** and **Valesin.**

Occasional use of combination pain relievers is probably not a problem. But the pharmacologist's bible, *Goodman and Gilman's The Pharmacological Basis of Therapeutics,* warns against prolonged use of pain relievers containing salicylates and either salicylamide or acetaminophen. The fear is kidney damage.[5] Popular pain relievers that contain aspirin and acetaminophen include **Duradyne, Excedrin Extra-Strength, Gemnisyn, Goody's Extra Strength** and **Goody's Headache Powder, Panodynes Analgesic, Presalin, Supac, Tri-Pain, Valesin,** and **Vanquish.**

Q. Is it possible to obtain willow bark and use this for its aspirinlike effects like the Indians did? If so, where would you get it?

A. Check with your local health food store. It is not something readily available from pharmacies. Interest in herbal remedies is skyrocketing. Not surprisingly, some enterprising naturalists have thought to market ground up willow bark. The active ingredient in willow bark is salicin, otherwise known as salicylic acid. We're not quite sure why you would want to go au naturel, though. The original users of such herbal products complained quite bitterly (literally, because salicin is bitter tasting) that they were irritating to the stomach. Willow bark is not likely to afford the same degree of heart attack and stroke prevention as regular aspirin.

References

1. The Multicenter Salsalate/Aspirin Comparison Study Group. ''Does the Acetyl Group of Aspirin Contribute to the Antiinflammatory Efficacy of Salicylate Acid in the Treatment of Rheumatoid Arthritis?'' *Journal of Rheumatology* 1989; 16: 321–327.
2. ''An Effective Arthritis Analgesic.'' *Modern Medicine* 1988; 56 (Aug.):41.

3. Clinical News. "CMT: An Effective Arthritic Analgesic."
   Modern Medicine 1988; 56 (Aug.): 41.
4. Van Tyle, W. Kent. "Internal Analgesic Products," in Feld-
   mann, Edward G., et al., eds. *Handbook of Nonprescription
   Drugs, 9th ed.* Washington, D.C.: American Pharmaceutical
   Association, 1990, pp. 68–69.
5. Gilman, Alfred G., et al., eds. *Goodman and Gilman's The
   Pharmacological Basis of Therapeutics, 8th ed.* New York:
   Pergamon Press, 1990, p. 647.

V

ALTERNATIVES TO ASPIRIN

CHAPTER 21

ACETAMINOPHEN (TYLENOL, ANACIN-3, ETC.)

Here's a little known fact for you. **Tylenol** (Acetaminophen) used to be available by prescription only. It was originally introduced as a children's elixir for fevers and pain in 1955. **Tylenol** didn't become available over the counter until 1960.[1] In its early days on the market it had a lackluster career. The American public was happy with aspirin and didn't see the need for something new. These days acetaminophen is a giant blockbuster hit in the multibillion-dollar pain reliever market.

There are so many acetaminophen brands out there, it is hard to keep track. Of course, **Tylenol** is still the best known. But there is also **Anacin-3**, generic **APAP, Aspirin Free Excedrin Dual, Bayer Select Maximum Strength Headache, Maximum Strength Backaid Pills**, and **Panadol**, to name just a few. There are also hundreds of multi-ingredient products—from cold remedies to nighttime pain relievers—that also contain acetaminophen.

Acetaminophen belongs to a category of drugs referred to as the coal tar analgesics. These compounds were discovered through chemical manipulation of para-aminophenol, which was related to the coal tar dye, aniline. The first of the lot was acetanilide, developed in 1886 and sold as **Antifebrin**. It turned out to be far too toxic and ended up on the scrap heap of dead pharmaceuticals. What was thought to be a less toxic chemical cousin, phenacetin, was introduced in 1887. It became extremely popular, especially in APC tablets (aspirin, phenacetin, and caffeine), until it was banned in the 1980s because of kidney toxicity. Acetaminophen, known in much of the rest of the world as paracetamol, was developed in 1893, but languished until the 1960s.

Read on if you would like to discover some startling new information about both the benefits and the risks of acetaminophen.

❑   ❑   ❑   ❑

Q. Our doctor advised my husband to stop aspirin and use Tylenol because of internal bleeding. Is there some alternative he could use which would allow him to get aspirin's protection against heart attack and stroke? Does Tylenol have similar protective effects?

A. Acetaminophen (**Tylenol**) may be roughly comparable to aspirin in relieving headache pain and lowering a fever, but it does not affect the blood the way aspirin does. This is good if bleeding is a risk (such as during surgery), but it also means that acetaminophen won't protect against heart attacks or strokes. Your husband had best follow his physician's prohibitions against taking aspirin. His risks of hemorrhage must outweigh the benefits of heart attack prevention.

Q. In what ways is Tylenol (acetaminophen) a good substitute for aspirin and in what ways is it not? Are there benefits provided by Tylenol which aspirin does not provide?

A. For people with sensitive stomachs, acetaminophen (**Acephen, Aceta, Anacin-3, APAP, Aspirin Free Excedrin Dual, Bayer Select Maximum Strength Headache,**

Panadol, Tylenol, Valadol, etc.) represents a valuable alternative to aspirin. Not only is it roughly comparable in relieving the pain of a headache, muscle strain or sprain, and lowering a fever, acetaminophen may be much better for relieving the discomfort of osteoarthritis than anyone used to think.

Traditional medical wisdom stated that aspirin and other anti-inflammatory drugs like ibuprofen (**Advil, Bayer Select Pain Relief, Motrin IB, Nuprin**, etc.) relieved the symptoms of arthritis far better than acetaminophen. The reasoning went that acetaminophen only helped partially—against pain—but not against the inflammatory response responsible for pain. New research has shaken this dogma to its foundation.

An article published in the *New England Journal of Medicine* concluded that "in short-term symptomatic treatment of osteoarthritis of the knee, the efficacy of acetaminophen was similar to that of ibuprofen, whether the latter was administered in an analgesic or an anti-inflammatory dose."[2]

We are talking major heresy here. The idea that acetaminophen could relieve the discomfort of garden variety arthritis about as well as ibuprofen is nothing short of revolutionary. Patients received 4,000 mg of acetaminophen daily in divided doses (at meals or with milk, this would be like taking two **Extra Strength Tylenols** [500 mg each] four times a day.). This dose was compared to either a divided daily dose of 1,200 mg of ibuprofen (equivalent to six over-the-counter **Motrin IB** pills [200 mg each]) or 2,400 mg of ibuprofen (12 pills divided into four equal doses throughout the day). Surprisingly, all three regimens worked about equally well to control pain.

As exciting as this research may be, there are some cautions. First, the patients who were treated were suffering from mild to moderate osteoarthritis of the knee. Although it seems logical to assume that acetaminophen should work for fingers, hips, shoulders, and other joints, more research is necessary to confirm the benefits. Of greater concern is the dose and length of treatment. The investigators stressed that this was a short-term study of only four-weeks' duration. Longer studies are necessary to compare acetaminophen with aspirin and other anti-inflammatory agents.

The biggest concern we have has to do with the toxicity of acetaminophen. Many people assume **Tylenol** is much safer than aspirin, but that may not be true. While acetaminophen is far easier on the digestive tract than aspirin, it may cause more problems for the kidneys and liver, especially if taken in large doses for long periods of time.

We have known for years that phenacetin (the P in APC tablets) could cause kidney damage. This coal tar analgesic was once found in many popular pain relievers, including the highly successful **Empirin Compound**, which contained aspirin, phenacetin, and caffeine. But when the Food and Drug Administration concluded that phenacetin was far too risky, drug companies removed this ingredient from the market.

What does the phenacetin story have to do with acetaminophen? For starters, 75 to 80 percent of phenacetin is quickly turned into acetaminophen by the body (it is the primary breakdown product). Whether acetaminophen is also toxic to the kidney remains controversial.

In 1989 Dr. Dale Sandler, an epidemiologist at the National Institute of Environmental Health Sciences, reported that regular, long-term use of phenacetin had been linked to a fivefold increase in kidney problems. No surprise there. But in the same paper (published in the *New England Journal of Medicine*) she noted that repeated long-term use of acetaminophen was also associated with kidney damage (a roughly threefold increase).[3] Interestingly, aspirin did not appear to cause kidney disease.

Dr. Sandler emphasizes that occasional use of **Tylenol** or other acetaminophen products is not a cause for concern. She does worry about people who rely on these drugs for more than two weeks to treat pain: "Anyone who uses analgesics every day for more than a couple of weeks needs to see a doctor."[4]

It is also recognized that serious liver toxicity is a complication of large doses of acetaminophen taken for long periods of times. This is especially dangerous for people who like to indulge in alcoholic beverages on a regular basis. Acetaminophen overdose can cause fatal liver damage.

The bottom line is that while acetaminophen is gentle to the tummy, it can be a problem for kidneys and liver when used for long periods of time at maximal dosage. Anyone who considers such a program needs to be carefully monitored by a physician.

Q. Is it still advisable to give teenagers Tylenol instead of aspirin to prevent Reye's syndrome?

A. Tylenol is a safe way to control a fever or relieve a headache in teenagers or younger children. Concerns about aspirin and Reye's syndrome are still very real. Aspirin must never be given to kids if chicken pox or influenza is suspected. When they reach the age of 20 years old, you can relax and let them take aspirin.

❑   ❑   ❑   ❑

References

1. Bob Kniffen, Johnson & Johnson. Personal communication, Jan. 4, 1993.
2. Bradley, John D., et al. "Comparison of an Anti-inflammatory Dose of Ibuprofen, an Analgesic Dose of Ibuprofen, and Acetaminophen in the Treatment of Patients with Osteoarthritis of the Knee." *N. Engl. J. Med.* 1991; 325:87–91.
3. Sandler, D.P. "Analgesic Use and Chronic Renal Disease." *N. Engl. J. Med.* 1989; 320:1238–1243.
4. Sandler, Dale P. Personal communication, May 9, 1989.

CHAPTER 22

IBUPROFEN AND OTHER NSAIDS (NONSTEROIDAL ANTI-INFLAMMATORY DRUGS)

Ibuprofen (**Motrin**) was introduced to the United States as a prescription pain reliever and and arthritis medicine in 1974. It quickly became a physician favorite for treating sore muscles, arthritic joints, and sprained ankles. **Motrin** rose to the top of the doctor's hit parade of most-prescribed medicines.

In 1984 ibuprofen went over the counter and became an overnight sensation for people in pain. The market leader in the early going was **Advil**, with **Nuprin** in second place. These days there is lots of competition. **Motrin IB** is taking a huge slice of the pie. Then there is **Bayer Select Pain Relief, Excedrin IB**, and **Midol IB Cramp Relief Formula**.

Ibuprofen is an excellent anti-inflammatory drug. It can relieve the pain of a headache, as well as the discomfort of arthritis, tennis elbow, a backache, or menstrual cramps. Unlike aspirin, it is unlikely to provide much benefit in protecting against heart attacks or strokes. Ibuprofen can lower a fever about as well as aspirin and is available in children's formulations for this purpose.

Ibuprofen, like aspirin, can do a nasty number on your digestive tract. Indigestion, heartburn, nausea, stomach pain, and diarrhea are possible side effects. Ulcers, bleeding ulcers, and perforated ulcers are more serious adverse reactions. Ibuprofen may also be tough on kidneys, so people with a history of kidney problems or congestive heart failure must be extremely cautious if they take this drug. Ibuprofen may also reduce the effectiveness of certain blood pressure medicines. Always check with your pharmacist about interaction precautions if you take multiple medications.

If you are allergic to aspirin, you could well be allergic to ibuprofen. Hives, skin rash, fever, and elevated liver enzymes are symptoms of ibuprofen allergy. Visual changes should be reported to an ophthalmologist immediately. Although an uncommon side effect of ibuprofen, damage to the eye can be serious.

❏   ❏   ❏   ❏

Q. Is Nuprin really better than aspirin for menstrual cramps? How about sprains and minor injuries?

A. Ibuprofen (**Advil, Bayer Select Pain Relief, Excedrin IB, Midol IB Cramp Relief Formula, Motrin IB, Nuprin,** etc.) appears to be substantially better than aspirin when it comes to relieving menstrual cramps. Hormonelike chemicals called prostaglandins are responsible for a wide variety of life processes, including cell growth, metabolism, inflammation, and reproduction. They get labor started by initiating uterine contractions.

Women who suffer bad menstrual cramps may have abnormally high levels of prostaglandins. Ibuprofen and other anti-inflammatory agents (such as **Naprosyn, Ponstel, In-**

docin, etc.) seem especially effective at lowering the prostaglandins responsible for cramps and alleviating symptoms.[1,2,3] Aspirin and acetaminophen just do not do the job the way ibuprofen can.[4]

When it comes to sprains, strains, arthritis, headaches, and other minor hurts, aspirin and ibuprofen appear roughly comparable, though for dental surgery ibuprofen may be better than aspirin. The pain-relieving dosage range for ibuprofen is 200 to 400 mg and the effect should last four to six hours. There is no reason to exceed 400 mg unless you are trying to relieve the inflammation associated with arthritis.

Q. Is it safe to take aspirin and Advil together?

A. There is no logical reason to use ibuprofen and aspirin together. There shouldn't be any additional analgesic effect but there is substantial risk of stomach upset and ulceration. Don't do it.

Q. What other drugs can serve as substitutes for aspirin?

A. Prescription pain relievers can substitute for aspirin or ibuprofen. Some of these other anti-inflammatory agents include:

Brand	Generic
Anaprox	naproxen
Ansaid	flurbiprofen
Clinoril	sulindac
Dolobid	diflunisal
Feldene	piroxicam
Indocin	indomethacin
Lodine	etodolac
Meclomen	meclofenamate
Motrin	ibuprofen
Nalfon	fenoprofen

Naprosyn	naproxen
Orudis	ketoprofen
Ponstel	mefenamic acid
Relafen	nabumetone
Tolectin	tolmetin
Toradol	ketorolac
Voltaren	diclofenac

Q. I've always used Bayer aspirin for pain relief, whether the problem was a headache or stiffness in my fingers from typing at a keyboard too long. I recently dicovered Bayer Select Pain Relief containing ibuprofen and have found it helpful. Is one supposed to be better than the other for arthritis pain?

A. Aspirin and ibuprofen are both quite effective for relieving the pain and inflammation associated with arthritis. Ibuprofen works by blocking an enzyme that is responsible for the formation of hormonelike chemicals called prostaglandins. They play a very important role in pain sensations and inflammation. Because ibuprofen is more potent, milligram for milligram, you do not have to take as much to achieve the same level of relief. The usual dosage range is 200 to 400 mg of ibuprofen, whereas you would need at least 650 mg of aspirin for a similar result. Ibuprofen may also last a little longer in the body, allowing a dose to be taken every 6 hours.

Q. Will ibuprofen protect me against a heart attack the way aspirin does? If so, how much should I take?

A. Ibuprofen is not as effective as aspirin in preventing blood clots. There is no evidence that it can protect against heart attacks, strokes, and other cardiovascular problems.

Q. I've been taking ibuprofen for my arthritis, but my doctor said I should try something more powerful. He wrote a prescription for Voltaren. When the pharmacist

told me how much it would cost, I almost dropped my teeth. Is it really that much better than ibuprofen?

A. Voltaren and other prescription NSAIDs are just as effective in relieving arthritis pain and inflammation as ibuprofen or aspirin. The differences among the various drugs in this category have more to do with convenience than effectiveness. Side effects are also similar. Some people do find that one of these medications works better than the others, so you and your doctor might need to try out a few to find one that suits you best. If **Voltaren** is too expensive and you are getting relief from ibuprofen, ask your doctor if you can't stick with your cheaper choice.

❏   ❏   ❏   ❏

References

1. Budoff, Penny Wise. "Use of Mefenamic Acid in the Treatment of Primary Dysmenorrhea." *JAMA* 1979; 241:2713–2716.
2. Hanson, Frederick W., et al. "Naproxen Sodium in Dysmenorrhea." *Obs. and Gynecol.* 52:583–587, 1978.
3. "Drugs for Dysmenorrhea." *Med. Letter* 1979; 21:81–83.
4. Chan, W.Y. *Ann. Rev. Pharmacol. Toxicol.* 1983; 23:131.

A BRIEF HISTORY OF ASPIRIN

- **400 B.C.**   Hippocrates suggests chewing willow bark for fever.
- **1763**   Willow bark documented in medical literature for helping reduce fever and relieve the ague.
- **1853**   Aspirin (acetylsalicylic acid) first synthesized by Von Gerhardt . . . and promptly forgotten.
- **1898**   Aspirin rediscovered, purified, and stabilized by Felix Hoffmann at the Bayer AG Chemical Works.
- **1899**   Trade name registered to the Bayer company on March 6. Aspirin goes on sale in Germany.
- **1903**   Aspirin is accepted as a safe and effective remedy for backache.
- **1923**   Aspirin accepted as a safe and effective remedy for headache.
- **1933**   Aspirin accepted as a safe and effective remedy for arthritis.
- **1948**   Aspirin first used to prevent heart attacks.
- **1971**   Aspirin's mechanism of action is discovered by Sir John Vane.
- **1975**   Research proves that low-dose aspirin prevents heart attack in people with heart disease.

- 1978   Research proves that aspirin reduces the risk of stroke.
- 1982   Studies prove that aspirin reduces the risk of heart attack in high-risk men.
- 1988   Preliminary studies suggest that aspirin may aid gallstone treatment.
- 1989   Study reveals that low-dose aspirin taken every other day reduces the risk of heart attack in healthy men by nearly 50 percent.
- 1989   Preliminary research suggests that aspirin may slow the development of cataracts.
- 1990   Studies indicate that aspirin taken every other day reduces migraine attacks.
- 1991   Research shows that aspirin helps prevent colon and rectal cancers.
- 1991   Studies demonstrate that aspirin reduces the risk of heart attacks in women.
- 1991   Research proves that aspirin helps prevent hypertension during pregnancy and low birth weight in babies.
- 1991   Studies show that mini-doses of aspirin reduce the risk of strokes.
- 1992   Studies confirm that low doses of aspirin can dramatically reduce the risk of colorectal cancer.

PRODUCTS CONTAINING ASPIRIN, ACETA- MINOPHEN, OR IBUPROFEN

ASPIRIN

Product Name	Aspirin Content
Adult Analgesic ½ Halfprin	81 mg
Adult Analgesic Pain Reliever	400 mg
Alka-Seltzer	324 mg
Alka-Seltzer Extra Strength	500 mg
Alka-Seltzer, Flavored	324 mg
Anacin Caplets	400 mg
Anacin Tablets	400 mg
Anacin, Maximum Strength	500 mg
Arthritis Pain Formula	500 mg
A.S.A. Enseals	325 mg/650 mg
A.S.A. Suppositories	325 mg/650 mg
Ascriptin	325 mg
Ascriptin A/D	325 mg

Product Name	Aspirin Content
Ascriptin, Extra Strength	500 mg
Aspergum	228 mg
Aspirtab	325 mg/500 mg
Bayer Aspirin, Genuine	325 mg
Bayer Aspirin, Maximum	500 mg
Bayer Aspirin, Therapy	325 mg
Bayer Children's Chewable Aspirin	81 mg
Bayer Enteric Safety Coated	81 mg
Bayer 8-Hour Timed-Release	650 mg
Bayer Plus	325 mg
Buffaprin	325 mg/500 mg
Bufferin, Arthritis Strength Tri-Buffered Caplets	500 mg
Bufferin, Extra Strength Tri-Buffered	500 mg
Bufferin, Tri-Buffered	325 mg
Buffex	325 mg
Buffinol	324 mg
Cama Arthritis Pain Reliever	500 mg
Cope	421 mg
Dolcin	240.5 mg
Easprin (prescription only)	975 mg
Ecotrin, Regular Strength	325 mg
Ecotrin, Maximum Strength	500 mg
Empirin	325 mg
Extra Strength Bayer Plus	500 mg
Genprin	325 mg
Halfprin	165 mg
Magnaprin	325 mg
Magnaprin Arthritis Strength	325 mg
Measurin Timed-Release	650 mg

Product Name	Aspirin Content
Midol Caplets, Original Formula	454 mg
Midol for Cramps Caplets, Maximum Strength	500 mg
Momentum Muscular Backache Formula	500 mg
Norwich Aspirin	325 mg
Norwich Extra Strength	500 mg
Norwich Enteric Safety Coated Aspirin	325 mg
Norwich Enteric Safety Coated Maximum Strength	500 mg
PAC	400 mg
Salabuff	324 mg
Sine-Off Sinus Medicine— Aspirin Formula	325 mg
Stanback Powder	650 mg
Stanback Max Powder	850 mg
St. Joseph Aspirin	325 mg
St. Joseph Adult Chewable Aspirin Low Dose	81 mg
Ursinus Inlay-Tabs	325 mg
Verin	650 mg
Wesprin Buffered	325 mg
ZORprin *(prescription only)*	800 mg

ACETAMINOPHEN

Product Name	Acetaminophen Content
Acephen Suppositories	120 mg/325 mg/650 mg
Aceta	325 mg/500 mg
Acetaminophen Liquid	32 mg/ml

Product Name	Acetaminophen Content
Acetaminophen Uniserts	120 mg/325 mg/650 mg
Actamin	325 mg/500 mg
Actamin Super	500 mg
Adult Strength Headache Relief Formula	325 mg
Alka-Seltzer Advanced Formula	325 mg
Allerest Headache Strength	325 mg
Allerest No Drowsiness	325 mg
Allerest, Sinus Pain Formula	500 mg
Aminofen	325 mg/500 mg
Anacin-3, Children's Chewable Tablets	80 mg
Anacin-3, Children's Liquid	30 mg/ml
Anacin-3, Infants' Drops	100 mg/ml
Anacin-3, Maximum Strength	500 mg
Anacin-3, Regular Strength	325 mg
Apacet Chewable Tablets	80 mg
Arthritis Pain Formula, Aspirin-Free	500 mg
Aspirin Free Anacin	500 mg
Aspirin Free Anacin P.M.	500 mg
Aspirin Free Excedrin	500 mg
Aspirin-Free Excedrin PM	500 mg
Aspirin Free Pain Relief	325 mg/500 mg
Banesin	500 mg
Bayer Select Maximum Strength Headache	500 mg
Bayer Select Maximum Strength Menstrual	500 mg

Product Name	Acetaminophen Content
Bayer Select Maximum Strength Night Time Pain Relief	500 mg
Bromo-Seltzer	325 mg
Bufferin AF Nite Time	500 mg
Congespirin for Children, Chewable	81 mg
Datril Extra Strength	500 mg
Dolanex	65 mg/ml
Dorcol Children's Non-Aspirin Fever & Pain Reducer	32 mg/ml
Excedrin Dual	500 mg
Excedrin P.M.	500 mg
Excedrin, Sinus	500 mg
Feverall, Children's Suppositories	120 mg
Feverall, Junior Strength Suppositories	325 mg
Feverall Sprinkle Caps	80 mg
Genapap, Children's Chewable	80 mg
Genapap, Children's Elixir	32 mg/ml
Genapap, Extra Strength	500 mg
Genapap, Infants' Drops	100 mg/ml
Genebs	325 mg
Genebs Extra Strength	500 mg
Halenol	325 mg
Halenol Children's Liquid	32 mg/ml
Halenol Extra Strength	500 mg
Liquiprin Children's Elixir	32 mg/ml
Liquiprin Solution	48 mg/ml
Maximum Strength Backaid Pills	1,000 mg
Meda-Cap	500 mg

Product Name	Acetaminophen Content
Meda-Tab	325 mg
Menoplex	325 mg
Menstra-Eze	325 mg
Midol Maximum Strength PMS Formula	500 mg
Midol Regular Strength	325 mg
Myapap Drops	100 mg/ml
Neopap Suppositories	125 mg
Oraphen-PD	24 mg/ml
Ornex	325 mg
Pain-Eze +	650 mg
Pamprin	400 mg
Pamprin, Maximum Strength Pamprin Cramp Relief Formula Menstrual Relief Tablets	500 mg
Panadol	500 mg
Panadol, Children's Chewable	80 mg
Panadol, Children's Liquid	32 mg/ml
Panadol, Infant's Drops	100 mg/ml
Panadol, Junior Strength	160 mg
Panadol, Maximum Strength	500 mg
Panex	325 mg
Panex 500	500 mg
Percogesic	325 mg
Phenaphen	325 mg
Premsyn PMS	500 mg
Redutemp	500 mg
Sinarest	325 mg/500 mg
Sinarest, No Drowsiness	500 mg
Sine-Aid Maximum Strength	500 mg

Product Name	Acetaminophen Content
Sine-Off Maximum Strength No Drowsiness	500 mg
Snaplets-FR Granules	80 mg
Sominex Pain Relief	500 mg
St. Joseph Aspirin-Free Infant Drops	80 mg/0.8 ml
St. Joseph Aspirin-Free Liquid for Children	80 mg/2.5 ml
St. Joseph Aspirin-Free Tablets for Children	80 mg
Suppap-120 Suppositories	120 mg
Synabrom	325 mg
Tapanol Extra Strength	500 mg
Tempra 3 Chewable Tablets	80 mg/160 mg
Tempra 1 Infant Drops	100 mg/ml
Tempra 2 Toddlers' Syrup	32 mg/ml
Tenol	325 mg
Tylenol Children's Chewable Tablets	80 mg
Tylenol Children's Drops	100 mg/ml
Tylenol Children's Elixir	32 mg/ml
Tylenol Extra Strength Caplets	500 mg
Tylenol Extra Strength Gelcaps	500 mg
Tylenol Extra Strength Tablets	500 mg
Tylenol Extra Strength Liquid	33.3 mg/ml
Tylenol Junior Strength	160 mg
Tylenol PM	500 mg
Tylenol Regular Strength Caplets	325 mg

Product Name	Acetaminophen Content
Tylenol Regular Strength Tablets	325 mg
Valadol	325 mg
Valorin	325 mg/500 mg
Valorin Super	500 mg

IBUPROFEN

Product Name	Ibuprofen Content
Aches-N-Pain	200 mg
Advil	200 mg
Bayer Select Pain Relief	200 mg
CoAdvil	200 mg
Genpril	200 mg
Excedrin IB	200 mg
Haltran	200 mg
Ibuprin	200 mg
Ibuprohm	200 mg
Ibu-Tab	200 mg
Midol 200	200 mg
Midol IB Cramp Relief Formula	200 mg
Motrin IB	200 mg
Nuprin	200 mg
Pamprin-IB	200 mg
Saleto-200	200 mg
Trendar	200 mg

COMBINATION PAINKILLERS

Product Name	ASA*	Acet**	Other Ingredients
Anodynos Tablets	420.6 mg		34.4 mg salicylamide 34.4 mg caffeine
Arthritis Strength BC Powder	742 mg		222 mg salicylamide 36 mg caffeine
BC Powder	650 mg		195 mg salicylamide 32 caffeine
BC Tablets	325 mg		95 mg salicylamide 16 mg caffeine
Buffets II	226.8 mg	162 mg	32.4 mg caffeine 50 mg aluminum hydroxide
Duradyne	230 mg	180 mg	15 mg caffeine
Excedrin Extra-Strength	250 mg	250 mg	65 mg caffeine
Gemnisyn	325 mg	325 mg	
Goody's Extra Strength	520 mg	260 mg	16.25 mg caffeine
Pain Reliever Tablets	250 mg	250 mg	65 mg caffeine
Presalin	260 mg	120 mg	120 mg salicylamide
S-A-C Tablets		150 mg	230 mg salicylamide 30 mg caffeine
Salatin Capsules	259.2 mg	129.6 mg	16.2 mg caffeine
Saleto Tablets	210 mg	115 mg	65 mg salicylamide 16 mg caffeine
Salocol Tablets	210 mg	115 mg	65 mg salicylamide 16 mg caffeine
Supac Tablets	230 mg	160 mg	33 mg caffeine
Tenol-Plus	250 mg	250 mg	65 mg caffeine
Trigesic Tablets	230 mg	125 mg	30 mg caffeine
Tri-Pain Tablets	162 mg	162 mg	162 mg salicylamide 16.2 mg caffeine
Valesin Tablets	150 mg	150 mg	150 mg salicylamide
Vanquish Caplets	227 mg	194 mg	33 mg caffeine

*aspirin
**acetaminophen

DRUG AND NUTRIENT INTERACTIONS WITH ASPIRIN

ASPIRIN CAN INTERACT WITH THE FOLLOWING DRUGS:

ACE Inhibitors	
Capoten (captopril)	**Vasotec** (enalapril)

Aspirin has been reported to reduce the effectiveness of these medications. They may not lower blood pressure or control congestive heart failure as expected. Merck has received several reports of such an interaction.

We heard from a retired judge taking Vasotec who had a dramatic jump in blood pressure (210/90) and a bad nosebleed when he took aspirin for a bad back. If you take an ACE inhibitor for hypertension, make sure you monitor your blood pressure before and after taking aspirin to see if there are any changes.

Activated Charcoal

Activated charcoal can "grab on" to a variety of drugs, including aspirin and similar compounds. Activated charcoal is available over the counter to reduce symptoms of intestinal distress due to gas. If taken at the same time as aspirin, activated charcoal may reduce the absorption and effectiveness of the pain reliever.

Alcohol

Scientists have long known that drinking alcohol within a day and a half of taking aspirin can substantially increase the damage both drugs do to the stomach lining. Alcohol also stimulates the production of acid, which makes matters worse.

In addition, swallowing aspirin an hour before downing about one and a half drinks can boost blood alcohol levels 26 percent over what would be expected from such a modest alcohol intake. Aspirin seems to deactivate a stomach enzyme called alcohol dehydrogenase that is responsible for breaking down some alcohol before it gets into the circulation. Women don't seem to have any significant amount of this enzyme, but a man unaware of this interaction could end up in serious trouble. The increased blood alcohol concentration could be enough to alter coordination and judgment.

Antacids

Advanced Formula
   DiGel
Alka-Mints
Alkets
ALternaGEL
Alu-Cap
Amitone
Amphojel
Camalox
Chooz
Dialume
Dicarbosil
Equilet
Extra Strength Maalox
Gaviscon
Gaviscon-2
Gaviscon Extra
   Strength Relief
   Formula
Gelusil

Gelusil M
Gelusil II
Maalox
Maalox TC
Magna Gel Tablets
Mallamint
Milk of Magnesia
Mylanta Tablets
Phosphaljel
Riopan
Riopan Extra
   Strength
Rolaids
Rolaids Calcium Rich
Titralac
Tums
Tums E-X Extra
   Strength
WinGel Tablets
etc.

Regular antacid use can reduce the amount of aspirin circulating in the bloodstream. This is no big deal for the occasional user of either aspirin or antacids, but someone
who needs large doses of aspirin should be monitored if
they must start or stop daily antacid therapy.

Anticoagulants

Coumadin (warfarin)   **Miradon** (anisindione)
Dicumarol

This interaction sets off all the alarm bells and sirens. Because aspirin is capable of thinning the blood, anyone taking one of these prescription blood-thinners must avoid aspirin unless their doctor has prescribed it and is monitoring blood clotting time closely. The additive action could lead to dangerous bleeding.

Anturane (sulfinpyrazone)

Aspirin interferes with the ability of this gout medicine to lower uric acid levels, and **Anturane** interferes with aspirin's capacity to alleviate gout. As little as 700 mg of aspirin has been known to counteract **Anturane's** effect almost completely.

Baking Soda

Sodium bicarbonate can make urine alkaline, leading to more rapid elimination of aspirin and similar compounds. This could reduce both benefits and side effects.

Benemid (probenecid)

Taking this gout medicine together with aspirin may keep either medicine from controlling uric acid buildup. Here's Here's a case where 1 + 1 = 0.

Beta Blockers

Blocadren (timolol)
Corgard (nadolol)
Cartrol (carteolol)
Inderal (propranolol)
Kerlone (betaxolol)

Levatol (penbutolol)
Lopressor (metoprolol)
Sectral (acebutolol)
Tenormin (atenolol)
Visken (pindolol)

These heart and high blood pressure medicines may be affected by aspirinlike drugs. Although good research is lacking, there is some preliminary data to suggest that the benefits of the beta blockers may be slightly diminished. That means blood pressure may not come down as far as expected when a beta blocker is taken with aspirin. Make sure you or your doctor monitor blood pressure carefully if these kinds of drugs are combined.

Bumex (bumetanide)

People with cirrhosis of the liver may not get the full effect of this diuretic if they are also taking aspirin. Check with the doctor.

Carbonic Anhydrase Inhibitors
(Glaucoma Medicine)

Daranide
  (dichlorphenamide)
Diamox
  (acetazolamide)

Neptazane
  (methazolamide)

This could be serious. Aspirin may increase blood levels of these glaucoma medicines, which could in turn lead to toxicity. Elderly people and those with kidney problems are especially susceptible.

Symptoms of confusion, fatigue, loss of appetite, incontinence, and metabolic changes have been reported when fairly high doses of aspirin were combined with these drugs. Check in with your ophthalmologist before mixing these kinds of medications.

Corticosteroids

Aristocort
  (triamcinolone)
Cortef (hydrocortisone)
Decadron
  (dexamethasone)

Delta-Cortef
  (prednisolone)
Deltasone (prednisone)
Medrol
  (methylprednisolone)
  etc.

These potent oral steroids can speed elimination of aspirin and similar drugs from the body. Consequently, a person on high doses of aspirin may not get the expected effect if they start taking a corticosteroid medicine too. On the other hand, going off a corticosteroid could boost aspirin levels much higher than anticipated, even at a steady dose.

Depakene (valproic acid)

This epilepsy medicine could become far more toxic if aspirin is taken with it. A person who really needs aspirin along with this antiseizure medicine should be monitored carefully for levels of free valproic acid in the blood and for elevated liver enzymes.

Diabetes Drugs, Oral

DiaBeta (glyburide)
Diabinese (chlorpropamide)
Dymelor (acetohexamide)

Glucotrol (glipizide)
Micronase (glyburide)
Orinase (tolbutamide)
Tolinase (tolazamide)

Combining aspirin or similar drugs with oral diabetes drugs can bring blood sugar down lower than expected. This effect has been reported at doses of around 3,000 mg daily of aspirin (nine or ten regular-strength tablets). Diabetics should take aspirin only under a doctor's supervision, with careful blood glucose monitoring.

Dilantin (phenytoin)

High doses of aspirin may raise the levels of **Dilantin** circulating in the bloodstream. In theory, this could increase both the effectiveness of and the potential for adverse reactions to this antiseizure medication.

Edecrin (ethacrynic acid)

People with cirrhosis of the liver and ascites (fluid in the abdomen) may not get the full effect of this diuretic if they are also taking aspirin. Check with your doctor.

Ergamisol (levamisole)

One preliminary report suggests that this drug used in cancer treatments may raise blood levels of aspirin if they are taken the same day. A further study did not confirm this interaction.

Heparin

Because both aspirin and **Heparin** work to prevent blood clotting, using them together increases the risk of dangerous bleeding. If someone receiving **Heparin** also needs aspirin, clotting (prothrombin time) must be monitored very closely.

Insulin

Type-II diabetics who inject insulin may find that blood sugar drops lower when they are taking aspirin. In some cases, people need a lower dose of insulin when they are on a regular aspirin therapy. Clearly, this interaction calls for careful blood glucose monitoring.

Lasix (furosemide)

People with kidney problems or cirrhosis and ascites (fluid in the abdomen) may not get the full effect of this powerful diuretic (water pill) if they are also taking aspirin. Check with the doctor.

Methotrexate

Folex   **Rheumatrex**
Mexate   etc.

Aspirin and other salicylates can increase the power—and also the side effects—of this strong medicine used to treat cancer, rheumatoid arthritis, and psoriasis. If you are taking **methotrexate** and *thinking* of taking aspirin, discuss it with your physician first. The dose of **methotrexate** might need to be adjusted.

NSAIDs

Advil (ibuprofen)
Anaprox (naproxen)
Ansaid (flurbiprofen)
Clinoril (sulindac)
Indocin (indomethacin)
Feldene (piroxicam)
Meclomen
  (meclofenamate)

Motrin (ibuprofen)
Nalfon (fenoprofen)
Naprosyn (naproxen)
Orudis (ketoprofen)
Ponstel
  (mefenamic acid)
Tolectin (tolmetin)
Voltaren (diclofenac)

Some people have found that these anti-inflammatory drugs are less effective at relieving pain from arthritis, bursitis, and so forth, when taken in combination with aspirin. This interaction is not well-documented and may vary from one person to another. Stomach irritation from these medications may be aggravated by aspirin.

Nitroglycerin

One study showed that nitroglycerin had a stronger effect in lowering blood pressure and increasing heart rate after people took 1 gm of aspirin. This could conceivably increase the possibility of headache or dizziness due to nitroglycerin.

Oral Contraceptives

Women taking birth control pills may not get the expected effect from aspirin or similar drugs. Using higher or more frequent doses may counteract this problem. Please check with your physician and pharmacist to get the amount right.

Spironolactone

Aldactazide   **Aldactone**

Spironolactone is a diuretic that works partly by helping the body kick sodium out in the urine. Aspirin and similar drugs can interfere with this action, although blood pressure control doesn't seem affected.

Vitamin C (ascorbic acid)

Aspirin seems to interfere with cells taking in this nutrient at normal levels. As a result, chronic aspirin users could, in theory, end up with less vitamin C in important places. This hasn't been reported as a clinical problem, though.

Aspirin may have a different effect depending upon how much vitamin C is available. One study showed that high doses of aspirin (3 gm/day) increased urinary excretion of the vitamin when the diet was low in ascorbic acid. When volunteers ate a diet rich in vitamin C, aspirin reduced their urinary levels of the nutrient. The amount of ascorbic acid in the blood did not vary with aspirin. Obviously, this is not a simple interaction.

References

Harkness, Richard. *Drug Interactions Guide Book*. Englewood Cliffs, NJ: Prentice Hall, 1991.

Johansson, U., and Akesson, B. "Interaction Between Ascorbic Acid and Acetylsalicylic Acid and their Effects on Nutritional Status in Man." *Int. J. Vitam. Nutr. Res.* 1985; 55(2):197–204.

Olin, Bernie R., editor-in-chief. *Drug Facts and Comparisons, 1992 ed.* St. Louis: Facts and Comparisons, 1992.

Roine, R., et al. "Aspirin Increases Blood Alcohol Concentrations in Humans After Ingestion of Ethanol." *JAMA* 1990; 264:2406–2408.

Tatro, David S., ed. *Drug Interaction Facts*. St. Louis: Facts and Comparisons, 1992.

DRUG INTERACTIONS WITH ACETAMINOPHEN

ACETAMINOPHEN CAN INTERACT WITH THE FOLLOWING DRUGS:

Activated Charcoal

Activated charcoal, the ingredient in gas masks, is incredibly good at "soaking up" some chemicals and may block their absorption into the bloodstream. In fact, poison control teams sometimes use it as part of the treatment of a drug overdose. Needless to say, a person taking activated charcoal capsules for flatulence may not get the expected effect from the acetaminophen pain reliever taken at the same time.

Alcohol

People who drink regularly risk liver damage if they also use acetaminophen on a regular basis. This is a potentially life-threatening interaction made worse by large doses of either compound.

Anturane (sulfinpyrazone)

Regular use of **Anturane** can make high doses of acetaminophen more hazardous to the liver.

Artane (trihexyphenidyl)

Artane may delay the action of acetaminophen when these drugs are taken together. Overall effectiveness should be unchanged.

AZT

Retrovir (zidovudine)

Acetaminophen increases the body's elimination of this anti-AIDS drug. Anyone planning to use acetaminophen while taking **Retrovir** should probably check in with the doctor for guidance.

Banthine (methantheline)

Banthine may delay the action of acetaminophen when these drugs are taken together. Overall effectiveness should be unchanged.

Barbiturates

Alurate (aprobarbital)
Amytal (amobarbital)
Butalbital
Butisol (butabarbital)
Fioricet
(acetaminophen,
caffeine, butalbital)
Fiorinal (aspirin,
caffeine, butalbital)

Gemonil (metharbital)
Lotusate (talbutal)
Mebaral
(mephobarbital)
Mysoline (primidone)
Nembutal
(pentobarbital)
Phenobarbital
Seconal (secobarbital)

Regular use of any of these barbiturates can reduce the effectiveness of acetaminophen. This combination carries the risk of liver damage if both drugs are taken for a sustained period of time.

Belladonna

Belladonna may delay the action of acetaminophen when they are taken together. Overall effectiveness should be unchanged.

Bentyl (dicyclomine)

Bentyl may delay the action of acetaminophen when these drugs are taken together. Overall effectiveness should be unchanged.

Beta Blockers

Blocadren (timolol)
Corgard (nadolol)
Cartrol (carteolol)
Inderal (propranolol)
Kerlone (betaxolol)

Levatol (penbutolol)
Lopressor (metoprolol)
Sectral (acebutolol)
Tenormin (atenolol)
Visken (pindolol)

This interaction is nothing to get too worked up about. **Inderal**, and possibly other beta blockers, may slow elimination of acetaminophen from the body. This could presumably increase or prolong the effects of the pain reliever, but probably not by much.

Cogentin (benztropine)

Cogentin may delay the action of acetaminophen when they are taken together. Overall effectiveness should be unchanged.

Dilantin (phenytoin)

Patients taking this epilepsy medicine may find that acetaminophen is somewhat less effective. In addition, regular use or high doses of acetaminophen are more likely to cause liver damage in those also taking **Dilantin**, **Mesantoin** (mephenytoin), or **Peganone** (ethotoin).

Isoniazid

INH   **Nydrazid**
Laniazid

A few cases of liver toxicity have been reported in patients taking both acetaminophen and isoniazid. Check with the prescribing physician.

Oral Contraceptives

Women taking birth control pills may have to be patient when taking acetaminophen for pain relief. It could take a little longer to start working and may not last quite as long, but overall effectiveness should be unchanged.

Pro-Banthine (propantheline)

Pro-Banthine may delay the action of acetaminophen when they are taken together. Overall effectiveness should be unchanged.

Rifampin

Rifadin   **Rimactane**
Rifamate

Acetaminophen may be slightly less effective when a person is taking this tuberculosis medicine.

Robinul (glycopyrrolate)

Robinul may delay the action of acetaminophen when they are taken together. Overall effectiveness should be unchanged.

Tegretol (carbamazepine)

This seizure medicine may reduce the effectiveness of acetaminophen. However, regular use of **Tegretol** can make an overdose of pain reliever far more damaging to the liver. Caution is advised.

References

Olin, Bernie R., editor-in-chief. *Drug Facts and Comparisons, 1992 ed.* St. Louis: Facts and Comparisons, 1992.

Tatro, David S., ed. *Drug Interaction Facts.* St. Louis: Facts and Comparisons, 1992.

INDEX

ABOUT THE AUTHORS

JOE GRAEDON, M.S. is a best-selling author, syndicated newspaper columnist, award-winning radio talk show host, health commentator for North Carolina Public Television, and lecturer at the University of North Carolina School of Pharmacy. He is president of Graedon Enterprises, Inc., a corporation providing pharmaceutical and health care information services.

Joe Graedon received his B.S. from Pennsylvania State University in 1967 and went on to do research on mental illness, sleep, and basic brain physiology at the New Jersey Neuropsychiatric Institute in Princeton. In 1971 he received his M.S. in pharmacology from the University of Michigan. Following his medical anthropologist wife Teresa to Mexico, he taught clinical pharmacology to second year medical students at the University of Oaxaca. While in Mexico he started work on *The People's Pharmacy* (St. Martin's Press, 1976; revised 1985), a popular book on medicines that would eventually go on to become a number one bestseller.

Joe has lectured at Duke University School of Nursing, University of California School of Pharmacy (UCSF), and University of North Carolina School of Pharmacy. He served as a consultant to the Federal Trade Commission from 1978 to 1983 and was on the Advisory Board for the Drug Studies Unit at UCSF from 1983 to 1989. He is a member of the Board of Visitors of the School of Pharmacy at the University of North Carolina, Chapel Hill. He is a member of AAAS, the Society for Neuroscience, the New York Academy of Science, and the American Medical Writers Association. For over a decade Joe contributed a regular column on self-medication for the journal *Medical Self-Care*. Joe is an editorial advisor to *Men's Health Newsletter*. His newspaper column, *The People's Pharmacy*, is syndicated nationally by King Features. *The People's Pharmacy* radio show won a Silver Award from the Corporation for Public Broadcasting in 1992.

Over the course of the last decade Joe has appeared on numerous national radio and television shows including *Donahue, Good Morning America, Today, Sally Jessy Raphael, Merv Griffin, The Tonight Show, Hour Magazine, The Home Show, Sonia Live, Cable News Network, American Magazine, Live with Regis and Kathie Lee, Everyday with Joan Lunden, The Larry King Show,* and *Geraldo.* Joe's features on health and pharmaceuticals are syndicated nationally to public television stations via Intraregional Program Service member exchange. He is considered the country's leading drug expert for consumers and is a popular keynote speaker on issues of pharmaceuticals, nutrition, and self-care. He lives in Chapel Hill, North Carolina, with his wife and coauthor Teresa and two children.

TOM FERGUSON, M.D., an award-winning self-help writer, is a graduate of Yale University School of Medicine. He was the first U.S. physician to specialize in self-help and self-care. His doctorate thesis at Yale was one of the first academic efforts to support self-care within the professional health care system.

He was founding editor of the journal *Medical Self-Care* and served for many years as medical editor of the *Whole Earth Catalog,* the *Whole Earth Review,* The *Essential Whole Earth Catalog,* and other *Whole Earth* publications. He is currently director of the Consumer Health Informatics Project at the National Wellness Institute, the University of Wisconsin-Stevens Point. (Consumer health informatics is the study of computer and telecommunications systems that provides laypeople with health information, advice, and support.)

Tom's articles have appeared in *Esquire, Playboy, American Health, Self, Glamour, Modern Maturity, Whole Earth Review,* and many other national magazines. Tom consults for some of America's leading health corporations and speaks regularly at leading universities and professional meetings.

He recently coordinated the nation's first meeting on Patient-Centered Medicine at the Commonweal Institute and the first national meeting on Consumer Health Informatics at the University of Wisconsin. He is a consultant on health trends to the U.S. Embassy in Tokyo and a member of the Board of Trustees of the University of Wisconsin's National Wellness Institute.

Tom has received the National Press Association's Distinguished Achievement Award and the Lifetime Extension Award for his writings "on the rapidly expanding area of self-help." His work was cited by author John Naisbitt in his book *Megatrends* as representing "the essence of the shift from institutional help to self-help."

TERESA GRAEDON, Ph.D., is a medical anthropologist and an author, syndicated newspaper columnist, and radio talk show host.

She received an A.B. from Bryn Mawr college in 1969, graduating magna cum laude. Graduate study at The University of Michigan included doctoral research on health and nutrition in Oaxaca, Mexico, and culminated in a Ph.D. in 1976. From 1982 to 1983 she pursued postdoctoral training in medical anthropology at the University of California, San Francisco.

Teresa has taught at Duke University. She serves as Joe Graedon's coauthor on their syndicated newspaper column, *The People's Pharmacy*, and has coauthor several books with him. She also cohosts their call-in radio show, *The People's Pharmacy*, which won a Silver Award from the Corporation for Public Broadcasting in 1992.